LIBERAL ARTS
COLLEGES

DAVID W. BRENEMAN

LIBERAL ARTS COLLEGES

Thriving, Surviving, or Endangered?

THE BROOKINGS INSTITUTION
Washington, D.C.

Copyright © 1994

THE BROOKINGS INSTITUTION

1775 Massachusetts Avenue, N.W., Washington, D.C. 20036

Library of Congress Cataloging-in-Publication data
Breneman, David W.
    Liberal arts colleges : thriving, surviving, or endan-
gered? / David W. Breneman.
        p.   cm.
    Includes bibliographical references and index.
    ISBN 0-8157-1062-3 (alk. paper)—ISBN-08157-1061-5
    (pbk.)
    1. Private universities and colleges—United States—Fi-
nance.   2. Education, Humanistic—Economic aspects—
United States.
    I. Title.
    LB2342.B74   1994
    378'.04'0973—dc20   93-46086
                                                              CIP

                9 8 7 6 5 4 3 2 1
The paper used in this publication meets the minimum requirements of the American National Standard for Information Sciences—Permanence of paper for Printed Library
Materials, ANSI Z39.48-1984

                Typeset in Times Roman

        Composition by Monotype Company, Inc.
                Baltimore, Maryland

        Printing by R.R. Donnelley & Sons, Co.
                Harrisonburg, Virginia

Foreword

PRIVATE LIBERAL arts colleges are among the oldest of American institutions, but their history has been marked by periodic concern about their ability to survive. These small colleges often provide undergraduate education of the highest quality, but their modest size, high cost, and heavy dependence on tuition revenue puts them at a competitive disadvantage with larger, state-subsidized universities. As higher education emerged from the relatively expansive years of the 1980s into the economically distressed 1990s, concern about the future of liberal arts colleges came to the forefront again. Can these small, labor-intensive colleges thrive, or will they wither? Will families be able—and willing—to pay the costs required for this type of education? Will the drift toward technical and professional studies doom colleges devoted to the seemingly less practical study of the arts and sciences?

The author, an economist and former college president, explores these and many other educational and economic issues in this book, a detailed analysis of more than 200 private liberal arts colleges. A central purpose of the book is to promote understanding of the unusual experience of the 1980s, a decade during which tuition rates rose sharply, colleges increased the aid they provided to students, and the curriculum evolved toward more professional undergraduate courses of study. What emerges is a nuanced assessment. Some colleges are thriving, most have survived, and a few are endangered.

The author received research assistance from four organizations: the Williams College Project on the Economics of Higher Education, the National Center for Higher Education Management Systems (NCHEMS), the College Board, and Harvard University. In particular, he would like to thank Michael McPherson, Morton Schapiro, Gordon Winston, and Anne Karabinos of Williams College; Dennis Jones and Paul Brinkman of NCHEMS; Donald Stewart, Jean Marzone, Ariel Foster, and Jim Cocoros of the College Board; and Martin Ahumada, Catherine Burack, Fred Galloway, Arthur Levine, Richard Murnane, Donna Plasket, Henry Rosovsky, and Judy Singer of Harvard University. Marybeth Ahearn provided research assistance early in the project, while Catherine Burack assisted on all data analyses and related research. Conversations with William G. Bowen of the Andrew W. Mellon Foundation, Fred Galloway of Harvard, Arthur M. Hauptman of Washington, D.C., and the comments of an anonymous reviewer were especially helpful in the development of the theory section in chapter 3, as were the writings of David Hopkins and William Massy.

Special thanks are offered to the officials of the 12 site-visit colleges, who provided extensive planning documents and related materials and gave generously of their time during the campus visits.

Edward O. Blews, Jr., president of the Association of Independent Colleges and Universities of Michigan, together with staff at the National Association of Independent Colleges and Universities in Washington, D.C., arranged in 1989 for the author to discuss the study with the State Association Executive Council, whose members subsequently helped in the selection of colleges included in the study. Jon Fuller, former president of the Great Lakes College Association and of the Council for the Advancement of Private Higher Education, gave valuable assistance early in the project. Charles L. Schultze and Henry J. Aaron directed the Brookings Economics Studies program during the research and provided significant assistance to the author.

The author also thanks the students, faculty, staff, trustees, and alumni of Kalamazoo College, Michigan, where he served as president from 1983 to 1989. Much that the author knows and values about the private liberal arts college stems from that rich experience.

Theresa Walker edited the manuscript, David Bearce verified it, Susan Woollen prepared it for typesetting, and Rhonda Holland compiled the index. Lisa L. Guillory, Sara C. Hufham, Paige Oeffinger, and Anita G. Whitlock helped to prepare the manuscript for production.

Financial support for the project was provided by the Andrew W. Mellon Foundation. The author thanks William G. Bowen and Roberto Ifill for their support and encouragement in all aspects of the work.

The views expressed in this book are solely those of the author and should not be ascribed to the organizations or persons acknowledged above, or to the trustees, officers, or staff members of the Brookings Institution.

BRUCE K. MACLAURY
President

December 1993
Washington, D.C.

Contents

Appendixes

Index

Tables

Figures

CHAPTER ONE

Introduction

MANY INDEPENDENT colleges thriving today can trace their origins back to the seventeenth and eighteenth centuries. Harvard College (now University) heads the list, dating to 1636, but other early colleges include St. John's, 1696; Salem, 1772; Dickinson, 1773; Hampden-Sydney, 1776; Transylvania, 1780; Washington and Jefferson, 1781; Franklin and Marshall, 1787; Williams, 1793; Bowdoin, 1794; and Union, 1795. Few business firms can point to such histories, and only a handful of churches and government organizations seem to be contenders for equivalent lengths of service. Indeed, the private liberal arts college stands out as one of American society's greatest success stories. Ironically, however, the literature on the private (or independent) college portrays a nearly unbroken history of concern for its survival. Are we looking at one of the hardiest of institutions, or one of the most fragile? Or, in some sense, are both attributes present? And what of the future of these institutions?

This volume examines the recent and changing financial circumstances of the independent liberal arts college in America, an institution uniquely important in the U.S. system of higher education. In this book financial and economic analyses will be intertwined with a discussion of educational purpose and mission to paint a more complete picture of the strengths and weaknesses of this type of college. We will see, for example, that the struggle for institutional survival in recent years has driven many of the less prestigious colleges to abandon or sharply scale back their original educational missions in the arts and sciences in order to teach professional subjects more strongly in demand. We will also see that cutbacks in the real value of federal financial aid, coupled with strong economic growth in the 1980s, gave rise to a successful strategy of expanding student aid through discounts in

1

tuition, thereby allowing private colleges to maintain enrollments. These are only two examples of the many ways in which economic factors impinge on educational activities, making it essential to understand the underlying economic forces influencing educational change.

I also briefly trace the relevant literature prior to the 1980s as a prelude to empirical analyses covering the past decade. The experience of higher education in the 1980s has deviated strikingly from the pattern forecast by economists and other analysts in the late 1970s. Rarely has a body of predictions been so wrong. Instead of a drop in enrollments, followed by college closures, as projected, the 1980s witnessed generally increased enrollments, sharply rising tuitions, and few college closures. The story of this recent decade has yet to be told in detail, a central purpose of this volume.

An understanding of the past should also prove helpful in looking ahead to the 1990s and beyond. If, as will be argued, the case for maintaining a strong group of liberal arts colleges within higher education is compelling, then it behooves us to pay attention to the forces operating on—and changing—them. For example, data presented in appendix A support the argument that more than 300 of the colleges listed by the Carnegie Foundation for the Advancement of Teaching[1] as liberal arts colleges have become something else—small professional schools with a liberal arts tradition but little of the reality of a traditional liberal arts institution.[2] Many of these colleges shifted curricular focus during the 1970s and 1980s to meet student demands and to maintain enrollments, with the changes occurring quietly and largely unnoticed, campus by campus. Without such changes, the closures forecast in the late 1970s might well have happened, and yet, in a meaningful sense, the country has still lost several hundred liberal arts colleges.

Given the failure of earlier forecasts about the future of various sectors of higher education, this book does not make a similar attempt at prediction. Instead, findings from site visits at twelve colleges— Bowdoin, Bradford, Colorado College, Dickinson, Fisk, Guilford, Hollins, Knox, Olivet, Union, Westmont, and Wittenberg—reveal the diversity of circumstances facing private colleges and offer information

1. Carnegie Foundation for the Advancement of Teaching, *A Classification of Institutions of Higher Education* (Princeton, 1987), pp. 31–40.
2. An early version of this argument is presented in David W. Breneman, "Are We Losing Our Liberal Arts Colleges?" *College Board Review*, no. 156 (Summer 1990), pp. 16–21, 29.

on how these schools are preparing for the future.[3] Common problems are noted, as are issues unique to each institution. No common future awaits private colleges as a group, and thus analyses must be done case by case. Although policy proposals are not my primary focus, suggestions for federal, state, and private actions are advanced, along with ideas for presidents and trustees to consider.

Why Study Private Liberal Arts Colleges?

Why is a book on the economic status of private colleges warranted? As a field of study, the economics of higher education has largely focused on the demand rather than the supply side of the education market, and economists often hold the view that little public interest inheres in the ebb and flow of particular colleges and universities. What does it matter if 50 or 100 private colleges fail financially as long as the demand for higher education is met by surviving institutions? What justification can there be for an economic study of a relatively small subset of the institutions that make up the universe of higher education?

To a considerable extent, my decision to study the private liberal arts college reflects my personal experience and values, although such conviction is not meant to detract from the value of other types of colleges and universities. (Indeed the diversity of American higher education is viewed almost universally as one of its glories.)

One of the most interesting and distinctive attributes of the liberal arts colleges included in this study is their commitment to their central educational missions. Unlike many colleges and universities in recent decades, they have refused to shift curricula toward more immediately marketable technological or vocational subjects. In fact one can almost view these colleges as standard bearers, holding out the promise and the reality of education for education's sake. Without them, American higher education would lose far more than simply places for some 260,000 undergraduates, a minuscule 2 percent of total enrollments. Ten new universities could absorb that population, but at the cost of a great loss of diversity in our educational system. The search to understand more fully how colleges that have resisted the pressure

3. See chapters 5 and 6 in this volume.

to emphasize professional education have survived, and what their prospects for the future are, is an intellectual challenge.

At their best, I believe that private liberal arts colleges provide the finest undergraduate education available in this country.[4] Importantly, these colleges are single-purpose institutions, with no rationale for existence beyond their capacity to educate undergraduate students. We do not rely on them for large-scale research, graduate or professional education, or public service beyond that which members of an intellectual community regularly offer their local area. By contrast, the other principal forms of higher education in this country, the university and the community college, are multipurpose institutions in which undergraduate education must compete with other activities for attention and resources. In the universities, research and graduate and professional education generally are accorded greater value in the incentive systems and reward structures that guide the allocation of faculty time and effort, while in the community college, vocational-technical training, remedial instruction, and various forms of community service activities vie with general education for resources and administrative support. To argue that multipurpose institutions can do a better job of undergraduate education than a college devoted solely to that purpose would require one to prove that the competing activities enhance, rather than detract from, undergraduate education, a view contrary to my experience.[5]

The small size of the typical liberal arts college, with perhaps 1,500 students, is a second factor of considerable educational importance. Coupled with a student-faculty ratio rarely higher than fifteen to one, the result is a smaller average class size than in a university or community college (particularly in the first two years), and greater student-faculty contact.[6] The university lecture class of several hundred students, heavily staffed with graduate student teaching assistants, is unknown in the small college. Prospective students and their parents make it abundantly clear that these considerations weigh heavily in their comparisons of the college and the university. Bright undergraduates in

4. There are, however, some students who will do better in universities than in colleges. For a significant number of students, though, a college is the better choice.

5. The case in favor of the university college is presented by Henry Rosovsky in *The University: An Owner's Manual* (W.W. Norton & Company, 1990), pp. 75–98.

6. Certain private universities, such as Princeton, pride themselves on providing ample faculty contact for undergraduates.

the college setting, especially in the sciences, may often work closely with faculty on research projects. In the university, such opportunities are normally reserved for graduate students. One result of these early laboratory experiences is the high proportion of liberal arts college graduates who subsequently earn Ph.D.'s, compared with peers who graduate from universities.

Faculty reward structures also vary among types of institutions in a way that favors excellent teaching in the liberal arts college. With undergraduate education the sole purpose of the liberal arts college, naturally faculty will be selected and rewarded primarily for their ability as teachers. Indeed, many young doctorates earned their B.A. degrees in liberal arts colleges and found that experience highly rewarding. Eventually these students create a steady supply of willing candidates for teaching positions in these same schools, even though salaries tend to be lower than in the universities, and opportunities for research are limited.

Selective admissions and residential life also figure importantly in a study of the quality of institutions of higher education. A handful of liberal arts colleges are among the most selective institutions of higher education, but so are a handful of universities, public and private. Similarly, full-time, residential attendance is hardly limited to the college, as many more students nationally live in residence at universities. Nonetheless, while part-time commuting students are found in small numbers in many colleges, a nonresidential college is almost a contradiction in terms; such students are far more common, however, in universities, and they dominate the community college setting.

These impressionistic comments do find support in the research literature. In one of the most thorough examinations of the effects of type of college on student attitudes, values, and knowledge, Alexander Astin reported in 1977 on the findings from the first ten years of the annual Cooperative Institutional Research Program that he directs at UCLA.[7] In summarizing his findings on the impact of size, he wrote:

> Students at large institutions are less likely to interact with faculty, to get involved in campus government, to participate in athletics, to become involved in honors programs, and to be verbally aggressive in their classrooms. The only exception is student involvement in demonstrations, which is increased at large institutions. This latter finding is

7. Alexander W. Astin, *Four Critical Years: Effects of College on Belief, Attitudes, and Knowledge* (Jossey-Bass Publishers, 1977).

consistent with the positive effect of size on liberalism and on support for student autonomy. Large institutions also reduce the student's chances of achieving in areas of leadership, athletics, journalism, and theater.[8]

With regard to public versus private control of an institution, he noted:

> Attending a private institution greatly increases the student's chances of interacting with faculty, participating in campus government, becoming familiar with instructors in the major field, and being verbally aggressive in classes. Students at private colleges are also more satisfied with classroom instruction, faculty-student contacts, closeness to faculty, and the institution's reputation. Students at public colleges are somewhat more satisfied with the administration, variety of the curriculum, and emphasis on social life. Most of these effects on satisfaction are attributable to the smaller size of private colleges.[9]

A less positive view of the effects of type of college on student development has recently been put forward in a comprehensive study.[10] After reviewing countless studies on college effects, the authors reach the following conclusions on the relative insignificance of "between-college effects":

> The weight of evidence may well reflect the fact that the dimensions along which American colleges are typically categorized, ranked and studied (such as size, type of control, curricular emphasis, and selectivity) are simply not linked with major differences in *net* impacts on students. To be sure, there are clear and unmistakable differences among postsecondary institutions in a wide variety of areas, including size and complexity, control, mission, financial and educational resources, the scholarly productivity of the faculty, reputation and prestige, and the characteristics of the students enrolled. At the same time, however, American colleges and universities also resemble one another in a number of important respects. . . . [They] do in fact produce essentially similar effects on students, although the "start" and "end" points may be very different across institutions.[11]

While there are well-known methodological difficulties in detecting such "between-college effects,"[12] nonetheless, the evidence favoring small private colleges is not unambiguously supported by the literature.

8. Astin, *Four Critical Years*, p. 230.
9. Astin, *Four Critical Years*, pp. 231–32.
10. Ernest T. Pascarella and Patrick T. Terenzini, *How College Affects Students* (Jossey-Bass Publishers, 1991).
11. Pascarella and Terenzini, *How College Affects Students*, p. 589. Emphasis in original.
12. Zelda Gamson, "How College Affects Students: Findings and Insights from Twenty Years of Research," *Change*, vol. 23 (November–December 1991), p. 50.

Other effects, however, including the role of private colleges in the education of scientists, have been noted for many years.

In the early 1950s, a path-breaking work that documented the central role of small, private colleges in producing graduates who subsequently earn doctoral degrees in the sciences was published.[13] This work was updated in 1985 in a report published by Oberlin College.[14] Data for the Oberlin report were collected from 48 private liberal arts colleges selected on the basis of several measures of productivity in training and research in science. In the introduction, S. Frederick Starr, president of Oberlin, summarized the findings as follows:

> Leading liberal arts colleges rank at or near the top of all American institutions of higher education—including multiversities and major centers of research—in the training of scientists. . . . this success is due significantly to the close link between teaching and faculty research that exists on such campuses. . . . the premier colleges have been nearly immune to the erosion of student interest in science that has recently afflicted major research universities and the nation. Finally, [data] show that this record of accomplishment has been financed mainly by the institutions themselves and by tuition payments, the level of federal support going to science programs in liberal arts colleges having diminished even as support for university centers has grown. In other words, this report indicates that leading liberal arts colleges are not only exceptionally productive in the natural sciences but also relatively cost effective.[15]

The findings of the Oberlin report were reaffirmed in research conducted by Carol H. Fuller, who computed productivity ratios for all undergraduate colleges and universities based on the number of bachelor's recipients who subsequently earned a Ph.D. She found that small liberal arts colleges were outstanding in productivity across Ph.D. fields.[16]

Another simple measure of institutional productivity is the degree-completion rate, defined as the percentage of entering students who

13. R.H. Knapp and H.B. Goodrich, *Origins of American Scientists* (University of Chicago Press, 1952).

14. David Davis-Van Atta, Sam C. Carrier, and Frank Frankfort, *Educating America's Scientists* (Oberlin, Ohio: Office of the Provost, Oberlin College, 1985). This report was disseminated through a conference at Oberlin on "The Future of Science at Liberal Arts Colleges."

15. Davis-Van Atta, Carrier, and Frankfort, *Educating America's Scientists,* pp. 1–2.

16. Carol H. Fuller, "Ph.D. Recipients: Where Did They Go to College?" *Change,* vol. 18 (November–December 1986), pp. 42–44.

receive a bachelor's degree within six years after starting college. Drawing on data collected by the Department of Education's survey, *High School and Beyond*, of 28,000 high school seniors in 1980, Oscar Porter found that 54.2 percent of the full-time students who enrolled directly after high school in independent colleges and universities completed their degrees in six years, compared with 42.7 percent of comparable students in public institutions.[17] Porter also found that four years after high school (often assumed to be the norm for college completion), only 15 percent of all students had earned degrees, while more than 25 percent of those in independent colleges and universities had finished. These degree productivity figures can be expressed in another way by noting that independent institutions enroll 21 percent of all undergraduates but produce 33 percent of all baccalaureate degrees.[18]

Ernest Pascarella and Patrick Terenzini also show that private institutions graduate a higher percentage of their students than do their public counterparts and have a "net positive influence . . . on plans for attending graduate school and overall . . . educational attainment."[19] When this fact is connected to their observation that simply graduating from college—any college—is the most significant effect on later achievement, including income, then both the higher rates of degree completion and shorter time taken to earn a degree emerge as principal advantages bestowed by private institutions.[20]

Furthermore, the enrollment at private colleges and universities belies the often-expressed view that these institutions serve only the children of wealthy, majority families. The National Institute of Independent Colleges and Universities reports that the proportion of minority students enrolled in state and in independent four-year institutions is similar in both sectors—17.8 percent in public and 18.2 percent in private colleges.[21] Furthermore, "Independent colleges and universities enroll more than twice as many students from families earning less

17. Oscar F. Porter, "Undergraduate Completion and Persistence at Four-Year Colleges and Universities," National Institute of Independent Colleges and Universities, Washington, D.C., 1990, p. vii.

18. National Institute of Independent Colleges and Universities, "Independent Colleges and Universities: A National Profile" (Washington, 1992), p. 2.

19. Pascarella and Terenzini, *How College Affects Students*, p. 376–77.

20. I am indebted to Carol H. Fuller of the National Institute of Independent Colleges and Universities for this point.

21. National Institute, "Independent Colleges and Universities," p. 3.

than $30,000 a year as from families earning more than $75,000 a year. The median family income of students in state and independent four-year institutions is identical—$36,000."[22]

As these data suggest, many private colleges and universities have been deeply committed to enhancing access to higher education by minority students and students from low-income families. Indeed, most private colleges have spent generously of their own institutional funds for scholarships and grants for those students who could otherwise never afford a private education. Nonetheless, the percentage of African-American students enrolled at most of the colleges in this study is minuscule (less than 5 percent), a troubling fact for students, faculty, administrators, trustees, and other supporters who see the educational and social need for increased diversity in the student body of these colleges.[23]

My final rationale for devoting a book to the future of private liberal arts colleges is rooted in a personal philosophy of education and view of the role of higher learning in our society. In recent years, the liberal arts have been under siege for economic and ideological reasons. On the economic front, degrees in liberal arts disciplines fell into disfavor with many college students, who read the labor market signals from the mid-1970s onward as calling for professional or technical training rather than broad education. Sarah E. Turner and William G. Bowen have documented a stunning drop in the percentage of bachelor's degrees awarded in the arts and sciences between 1968 and 1986, the share plummeting from 47 percent to 26 percent.[24] Most liberal arts colleges have felt the impact of this shift of demand away from their central offerings, and consequently many have made a comparable shift in their own curricula. As noted earlier, one of the reasons for this study is to examine the economic prospects of that set of colleges that did not make such an extensive change.

On the intellectual front, recent years have witnessed highly publicized battles within the academy, particularly in the humanities and social sciences, over the proper content of the liberal arts curriculum. First brought to wide attention by Allan Bloom's dyspeptic volume, *The Closing of the American Mind*, the outpouring of criticism directed

22. National Institute, "Independent Colleges and Universities," p. 2.
23. Demographic data bearing on this issue are presented in appendix A.
24. Sarah E. Turner and William G. Bowen, "The Flight from the Arts and Sciences: Trends in Degrees Conferred," *Science*, October 26, 1990, p. 517.

at faculty who are perceived to be ideologically motivated in their efforts to broaden the accepted canon has been startling to behold.[25] Although liberal arts colleges for the most part have not been at the forefront of these curricular struggles (the debate at Stanford University captured the most press attention), they have not been immune from its fallout.

Within these two crosscurrents, the position I want to stake out is the value of pure intellectual endeavor, represented at its best in the leading liberal arts colleges and universities. Most colleges and universities in this country cannot and perhaps should not resist the economic pressure to offer course work that provides skills needed in the immediate labor market; only the most prestigious colleges and universities have sufficient drawing power to resist these practical pressures. And yet, this relative handful of leading institutions sets the educational standard against which higher education is measured. Students at these institutions have the freedom and opportunity to spend four years immersing themselves in the best that has been written or produced in literature, science, history, philosophy, mathematics, and art; for our society, our culture, to have any ultimate meaning and value, those pursuits must be kept alive and nurtured as the heart of higher learning.[26] By their very nature, true liberal arts colleges are devoted to that task.

The current academic debates over what should be taught in a liberal arts program are fitting and proper intellectual matters, in no way contradictory to the essence of an excellent college.[27] No curriculum remains static, nor should it; new knowledge, new fields of learning, new emphases have marked the history of higher education and will continue to do so. We should worry only when the spark of learning

25. Allen Bloom, *The Closing of the American Mind* (Simon and Schuster, 1987). Recent entries into the fray over the curriculum include Dinesh D'Souza, *Illiberal Education: The Politics of Race and Sex on Campus* (Free Press, 1991); Roger Kimball, *Tenured Radicals: How Politics Has Corrupted Our Higher Education* (Harper & Row, Publishers, 1990); and Paul Berman, ed., *Debating P.C.: The Controversy over Political Correctness on College Campuses* (Dell Publishing, 1992).

26. For elegant development of this idea, see Jaroslav Pelikan, *The Idea of the University: A Reexamination* (Yale University Press, 1992); and Francis Oakley, *Community of Learning: The American College and the Liberal Arts Tradition* (Oxford University Press, 1992).

27. An excellent discussion of this topic is found in Amy Gutmann, ed., *Multiculturalism and "The Politics of Recognition": An Essay by Charles Taylor* (Princeton University Press, 1992), pp. 3–24.

for its own sake is extinguished, a danger inherent in a steadily growing emphasis on career and vocational studies.

Defining Liberal Arts Colleges

The Carnegie Foundation's 1987 classification of institutions of higher education is widely used, identifying by name 540 private liberal arts colleges and dividing them into two groups, Liberal Arts I (140 colleges) and Liberal Arts II (400 colleges).[28] The definition of these categories is as follows:

> Liberal Arts Colleges I: These highly selective institutions are primarily undergraduate colleges that award more than half of their baccalaureate degrees in arts and science fields.
>
> Liberal Arts Colleges II: These institutions are primarily undergraduate colleges that are less selective and award more than half of their degrees in liberal arts fields. This category also includes a group of colleges that award *less* than half of their degrees in liberal arts fields but, with fewer than 1,500 students, are too small to be considered comprehensive.[29]

At the beginning of this study I had planned to include all 540 private colleges in the Liberal Arts I and II categories of the Carnegie Foundation classification. In time I became convinced, however, that I would have to develop my own definition of liberal arts and list of colleges.[30]

---

28. The Carnegie Foundation for the Advancement of Teaching classifies 32 institutions as public liberal arts colleges, two in Liberal Arts I, and 30 in Liberal Arts II. The institutional type, "public liberal arts college," has not thrived or found a niche in U.S. higher education; pressures on public colleges seem to force them to be multipurpose institutions.

29. Carnegie Foundation, *A Classification of Institutions of Higher Education*, p. 7.

30. My definition, which stresses content over process, subject matter over teaching method, is controversial and by no means accepted by all educators. See appendix A in this book for an earlier version of this argument in my "Are We Losing Our Liberal Arts Colleges?" and rejoinders and counterarguments. For case studies of five colleges undergoing this transition see Edward P. St. John, "The Transformation of Private Liberal Arts Colleges," *Review of Higher Education*, vol. 15 (Fall 1991), pp. 83–106. Furthermore, it is not my intention in this book to link the state of liberal learning with the status of and prospects for liberal arts colleges. We could lose all our liberal arts colleges, and liberal learning could continue in other sectors. I believe the quality of liberal education in that circumstance would be diminished, however, because the one institution exclusively devoted to such education would be gone.

Conceptually, liberal arts colleges represent both an educational ideal and an economic type.[31] Educationally, liberal arts colleges award the bachelor of arts degree, are residential, primarily enroll full-time students between 18 and 24 years of age, and limit the number of majors to roughly twenty to twenty-four fields in the arts, humanities, languages, social sciences, and physical sciences. They rarely enroll more than 2,500 students, and most enroll between 800 and 1,800 students. The education they provide might be described as preprofessional, for many students enroll in graduate or professional programs upon graduation, but the liberal arts college itself offers virtually no undergraduate professional education.

Economically, liberal arts colleges have revenue and cost structures that can be reliably and intelligently compared, for they derive from institutions with similar programs and purposes.[32] These colleges are struggling to survive by offering a curriculum that does not cater to current student concerns with the job market. By remaining true to an educational ideal, the liberal arts college must compete with universities that provide many more courses and majors, and a vast array of professional degrees in business, engineering, architecture, nursing, and education. Consequently, both an educational ideal and an economic rationale enter into my definition of a liberal arts college.

Although it was not possible to adhere to these ideals slavishly in making my selections, they did provide criteria that narrowed the original group in my study from 540 institutions to 212. Of the 140 private Liberal Arts I colleges included in the Carnegie classification, I have retained 129; of the 400 private Liberal Arts II colleges, I have retained 83. Clearly most of my changes were in Liberal Arts II.

The colleges I excluded from the Liberal Arts I group might be thought of as "liberal arts plus," for they are essentially small universities. For example, Drew University has a seminary and offers several doctoral programs; Willamette University has both law and M.B.A. programs; Lewis and Clark enrolls several hundred graduate students in several fields of study; Bucknell has a range of programs that go well beyond the liberal arts, including a broad array of engineering

31. For an excellent discussion of this educational ideal see Oakley, *Community of Learning*.

32. To maintain financial comparability, I excluded 12 extremely small colleges (enrollment less than 300); see appendix B for details.

majors; Hamline has both a law school and a graduate program in liberal arts.

I call the more than 300 Liberal Arts II colleges that I excluded from my study "liberal arts minus," for they are essentially small professional colleges with few liberal arts majors but usually with a liberal arts core and tradition. The acid test that I applied in excluding colleges in this category was the percentage of degrees awarded in nonliberal arts fields.[33] I eliminated any college that awarded more than 60 percent of its degrees in professional fields. In other words, if a college awarded as few as 40 percent of its degrees in the liberal arts, I kept it, but only 83 of the 400 Liberal Arts II colleges met that low measure (Appendix B provides more information on colleges excluded).

A different pattern emerged for the degrees awarded by Liberal Arts I colleges. Twenty-six of them awarded no professional degrees, and thirty-one awarded fewer than 10 percent professional degrees. Business and education accounted for most of the professional degrees in colleges that awarded 25 percent to 40 percent of their degrees in professional fields. Six of the Liberal Arts I colleges awarded more than 60 percent professional degrees—Carroll, Thomas More, Wartburg, Rockford, Mt. St. Vincent, and MacMurray—but I decided to retain them in the data set because of their Liberal Arts I status.

My criterion, the percentage of degrees awarded in arts and sciences rather than occupational or professional areas, drastically cut the number of colleges included in this book from 540 to 212. My definition of a liberal arts college stems directly from the earlier discussion of their role as institutions that educate rather than train. At some point, admittedly arbitrary, a college that is awarding most of its degrees in business administration, nursing, education, engineering, health professions, and communications is simply no longer a true liberal arts college. By my definition we are indeed losing many of our liberal arts colleges, not through closures but through steady change into a different type of institution.

---

33. With help from the National Center for Higher Education Management Systems (NCHEMS) in Boulder, Colorado, I arrayed each college's undergraduate degrees awarded in 1985–86 by liberal arts and professional fields, with professional defined to include business, engineering, education, nursing, computer science, and agriculture. I then rank ordered the colleges by the percentage of professional degrees they awarded.

The shift from liberal arts to professional studies in the past twenty years came about primarily because of a demand-driven response to changing student interests, caused by shifts in the labor market for college-educated talent. After decades of high rates of return to a college education, the economic payoff fell in the 1970s, partly because of reduced demand for college-educated labor and partly because of large numbers of baby boom cohorts graduating and entering the labor force.[34] Faced with large numbers of applicants for positions, personnel managers often used specific training credentials as one way to screen the applicant pool, and students lacking technical skills suffered in that process. Graduates with liberal arts degrees were increasingly forced to augment their general education with advanced professional degrees. The shift in enrollments from liberal arts to professional education, documented by Sarah Turner and William Bowen, began in the 1970s and may have only begun to bottom out in the early 1990s.

This book is not the place to pursue the complicated arguments about general education versus specific training as the wisest long-range strategy for students surveying an ever-changing labor market. High percentages of the graduates of the leading liberal arts colleges go on to earned advanced degrees, which suggests that the bachelor's degree for such students is one form of preprofessional education (though a different form from that provided by professionally oriented bachelor of arts programs). Whether viewed in this fashion or in its own right, however, an economic case for liberal education does exist, based on the general skills of reading, writing, thinking, and analysis that result from such education, and the constantly changing nature of the economy, which can easily render specific training obsolete. Gary Becker, in his path-breaking volume, *Human Capital*, acknowledged these factors when he wrote, "Incidentally, the long payoff period increases the advantage of an education that is useful in many kinds of future economic environments. If 'liberal' education were identified with such flexible education, as well it may be, there would be an important economic argument for liberal education, as well as arguments based on intellectual and cultural considerations."[35] Loren Pope, long-time director of the College Placement Bureau in Washington,

34. The story is well told in a widely read book by Richard B. Freeman, *The Over-Educated American* (Academic Press, 1976).

35. Gary S. Becker, *Human Capital: A Theoretical and Empirical Analysis with Special Reference to Education,* 2d ed. (University of Chicago Press, 1980), p. 190.

D.C., reaches the same conclusion from a less theoretical perspective, "The sum of my experience has kept me firmly in the company of the best minds in education who have always said that the small college, dedicated to a liberal education, is not just the wisest and most sensible, but the most practical. In a world in which most of tomorrow's jobs don't even exist yet, it is the only way, the truth, and the life. Today, even the specialists are being made converts; the people who hire them are seeing the light."[36]

Economic Issues Facing Liberal Arts Colleges

Many economic problems face private colleges in the years ahead. First, although the largest drop in the annual population of high school graduates is behind us, the numbers are projected to decline nationally through 1994 and then rise slowly through the balance of the decade.[37] Overall figures conceal substantial regional differences, however, with the western states and the southern and south-central region projected to increase by 46.6 percent and 16 percent respectively between 1986 and 2004. The northeastern and north-central regions are projected to lose graduates between those years, 4.7 percent and 8.3 percent respectively.[38] A disproportionate number of liberal arts colleges are located in those regions projected to lose high school graduates in the years ahead.

Second, the widely publicized increases in private college tuitions during the 1980s raise the specter that fewer and fewer families will be able or willing to pay $15,000 to $20,000 a year for a private college education. To counter that problem, many colleges have sharply increased institutionally funded scholarships, with growing amounts of aid awarded on the basis of merit. For the majority of colleges without large applicant pools, such scholarships amount to tuition discounts, meaning that the colleges cannot actually charge the posted price and maintain enrollments.[39] More and more often colleges are devoting as

36. Loren Pope, *Looking Beyond the Ivy League* (New York: Penguin Books, 1990), p. xiii.

37. Western Interstate Commission for Higher Education, *High School Graduates: Projections by State, 1986 to 2004* (Boulder, Colo., 1988), p. 9.

38. Western Interstate Commission, *High School Graduates*, p. 11.

39. See Michele N-K Collison, "Private Colleges Unveil Tuition Discounts and Loans to Woo Middle-Income Students," *Chronicle of Higher Education*, June 24, 1992, p. A27.

much as 20 percent of their total educational budgets to such aid, a percentage that has risen steadily in recent years at most colleges. Although most presidents would like to stop or slow the growth of that aid, they fear that without it the college would not be able to maintain enrollments in the intensely competitive market for students.

One reason that institutions have been forced to increase their support of student aid has been the decline in real terms of federal student aid and of some state student aid programs during the 1980s. Although federal policy during the 1970s explicitly acknowledged two objectives, access and choice, it seems in recent years that choice has been downplayed, if not forgotten. Problems such as student loan defaults, the large and growing amount of federal aid absorbed by students in the proprietary sector (where default rates are highest), and the growth of loans relative to grants are issues that worry private college presidents, for they threaten to undermine the value of, and political support for, federal aid to students.[40]

The ability to compete for new faculty and to retain excellent faculty is a growing concern for many small colleges. Between the mid-1970s and 1990, most academic fields were marked by an excess supply of Ph.D.'s, and the private colleges have benefited from this buyer's market. The supply-demand balance for Ph.D.'s may shift the other way in the 1990s, however, exposing many small colleges to intense competition from wealthier universities for assistant and associate professors.[41] To remain competitive, colleges may be forced to raise salaries sharply and reduce teaching loads, putting more pressure on instructional costs, institutional budgets, and the student-faculty ratio that is a distinguishing feature of the liberal arts college.

The environment for fund-raising and the growing dependence on gifts for operating purposes reflect other concerns. Most private colleges are in a fund-raising campaign, have just finished one, or are planning the next one. Most of these colleges have never been able to run on tuition and endowment revenue alone, and the stakes rise yearly as campaign goals soar to new highs. Tax policy has an obvious bearing on this issue, as does the competitive environment for charitable

40. College Board, "Trends in Student Aid: 1982 to 1993," New York, September 1993.

41. William G. Bowen and Julie Ann Sosa, *Prospects for Faculty in the Arts and Sciences: A Study of Factors Affecting Demand and Supply, 1987 to 2012* (Princeton University Press, 1989).

support. Will these colleges be successful in raising the ever-growing amounts that they need to balance their budgets?

Finally, private colleges face growing competition with the public sector of higher education—for students, donor support, and political and community backing. This competition is nothing new, but it promises to take on critical importance in the decade ahead. Public universities are perfectly capable of creating honors colleges that mimic the best features of the private college, are much more involved in private fund-raising than ever before, and have the enormous benefit of state-subsidized tuition levels. Universities, public and private, are able to offer a much broader array of courses for undergraduates, including studies in the professional and technical fields that promise more immediate payoff in the labor market. Many presidents worry that private colleges may be rendered marginal, too small in numbers and enrollments to be taken seriously by policymakers at the corporate, state, or federal levels. The current focus on higher education's role in economic development and national competitiveness, for example, has largely bypassed the liberal arts college.

This litany of woes would be misleading, however, if mention were not made of the harsh effect of state budget cuts in the past three years on many public colleges and universities. The recession of the early 1990s has produced remarkable reductions in state appropriations for higher education, including cuts between 1989–90 and 1991–92 of 28 percent in Massachusetts, 17 percent in Rhode Island, 13 percent in New York, and 5 percent each in Florida and Mississippi.[42] As noted earlier, cuts of this size in state appropriations usually result in sharp increases in public tuition, thus reducing the price differential between a state's public and private colleges. Since the research for this book was started in 1989, the most striking economic change has been the reduction in appropriations for public universities in many states, indirectly reducing the competitive pressures on independent colleges. The recession has had a dampening effect on private colleges too and has done nothing to ease the other economic problems just discussed; nonetheless, the private sector has been spared the disheartening impact of abrupt revenue loss, an ironic benefit of financial independence from the state.

42. A. Flint, "State Public College System Staggers Amid Funding Cuts," *Boston Globe*, June 7, 1992, pp. 1, 22–23.

Organization of the Book

While this volume does not cover each of the economic issues mentioned in comparable depth, it does provide insight into the economic and financial forces operating on the institutions included in the study. Appendix A presents the criteria used to identify the 212 colleges that, by my definition, are still properly called liberal arts colleges. These 212 colleges are subdivided into groups defined by measures of financial wealth and recruitment strength in the enrollment market; financial analyses in chapters 3 through 5 follow these groupings in order to assess trends at the strongest and weakest ends of the continuum and determine whether the strongest colleges are becoming stronger and the weakest weaker (or vice versa), as well as the direction in which the institutions all along the spectrum are heading.

Chapter 2 contains an overview of the financial history of private colleges, examining trends from the mid-1950s through the 1970s. These were rich years in growth and development in higher education and in the depth of thought devoted to financing policies. The late 1970s and early 1980s witnessed numerous reports forecasting enrollment decline and severe financial problems for colleges in the 1980s, forecasts that proved wide of the mark. The striking contrast between the forecasts and the reality of the past decade has yet to be fully explained. Achieving a better understanding of what happened to these colleges in the 1980s and why is a central purpose of this book.

Chapter 3 examines enrollment, tuition, and financial aid, three subjects integrally connected and vital to the well-being of the private college. The chapter discusses the intricate financial relationship between the official tuition price and the amount of nonendowed financial aid offered, whether on the basis of need, merit, or some combination of the two. The rate of increase of "unfunded student aid" in most colleges seriously concerns many financial officers, presidents, and trustees. The correct way to view such aid in most colleges is as a discount from the posted price, for all that a college is doing when it makes such an offer is agreeing to accept the student at a lower rate of tuition. I believe that administrators in many colleges conceptualize the relationship between tuition and aid incorrectly and worry excessively about the growing share of accounting expenditures devoted to discounts. An alternative way of viewing the relationship in terms of net tuition revenue is presented, together with financial data comparing the growth of net tuition revenue with college expenditures.

Chapter 4 broadens the financial analysis by comparing sources and uses of funds for 181 of the colleges for fiscal years 1979 and 1989. By examining trends in revenues and expenditures we gain a better understanding of the differential effects of economic forces bearing on these colleges during the 1980s. Additional analyses examine financially stronger and weaker colleges, women's colleges, black colleges, and religiously affiliated colleges.

Chapter 5 discusses the recent experiences and planning activities of 12 colleges selected for site visits during the winter and spring of 1992. The colleges visited—Bowdoin, Bradford, Colorado College, Dickinson, Fisk, Guilford, Hollins, Knox, Olivet, Union, Westmont, and Wittenberg—are located in different states and offer reasonable coverage of the range of financial strength and drawing power found in private colleges.

Chapter 6 draws together the various strands of earlier discussions, highlighting and evaluating issues that have emerged as critically important to liberal arts colleges. A brief assessment of each of the 12 colleges visited is presented, giving the reader a sense of the future that each one faces.

CHAPTER TWO

A Brief Financial History

ALTHOUGH A NUMBER of American colleges are more than two hundred years old, many others have failed. As many as 700 colleges have been created and gone out of existence. One reason for the persistent concern about the survival of small, private colleges is grounded in the reality of past failures.[1] In the American "system" of higher education, small independent colleges are the most vulnerable institutions; often lacking sizable endowments, heavily dependent on tuition, and without direct support from government, these colleges can fail if times are hard enough.

Furthermore, their role has steadily declined over time, as other institutions have emerged as dominant forces in higher education. Starting from a position of unchallenged leadership, undergraduate liberal arts colleges enrolled two-thirds of all students in higher education at the turn of this century.[2] Even by that time, however, private colleges were facing a severe educational challenge from the newly developing universities that stressed research and the creation of new knowledge.[3] Seen from the heights of this powerful new institution, the liberal arts college seemed irrelevant and insignificant, destined to disappear. Historian Frederick Rudolph writes:

> President Harper of Chicago, at the turn of the century, expected three out of four existing colleges to be reduced to the status of academies or modified into junior colleges. President Butler of Columbia was convinced that if the American college was to be saved, it would have to reduce

1. Allan O. Pfnister, "The American Liberal Arts College in the Eighties: Dinosaur or Phoenix?" in National Institute of Education, *Contexts for Learning: The Major Sectors of American Higher Education* (Department of Education, 1985), p. 52.
2. Pfnister, "The American Liberal Arts College," p.48.
3. This story is told magnificently in Laurence R. Veysey, *The Emergence of the American University* (University of Chicago Press, 1965).

its course of study to two or three years. David Starr Jordan of Stanford looked into his crystal ball in 1903 and decided that "as time goes on the college will disappear, in fact, if not in name. The best will become universities, the others will return to their places as academies."[4]

In the face of such real or perceived threats, 150 college presidents convened in Chicago in 1915 to found the Association of American Colleges for the "promotion of higher education in all its forms, in the independent and denominational colleges in the United States."[5]

Subsequent events proved the earlier forecasts of demise to be extreme, but private colleges have been rendered increasingly marginal during this century as public universities and community colleges have grown dramatically in size and number. In 1955 liberal arts colleges still accounted for nearly 40 percent of all institutions—732 out of 1,854—and enrolled 26 percent of all students in that year.[6] By 1970, 689 private colleges—24 percent of the nation's 2,837 institutions— enrolled only 7.6 percent of all students. By 1987, the Carnegie Foundation identified 540 out of 3,389 institutions (16 percent) as private liberal arts colleges, with only 4.4 percent of total enrollments.[7] While the apocalyptic vision of the early university presidents did not come to pass, it is hard to argue with the judgment that, by 1990, the small private college had become a much diminished part of the educational landscape.

The 1950s and 1960s—Golden Years?

The tone of discussion in the mid-1950s can be seen best in the pages of an obscure, but fascinating, document entitled *The Sixty College Study: A Second Look*.[8] This effort was a four-year follow-up

4. Frederick Rudolph, *The American College and University: A History* (Alfred A. Knopf, 1962), p. 443.

5. Mark H. Curtis, "Crisis and Opportunity: The Founding of AAC," in *Enhancing, Promoting, Extending Liberal Education: Association of American Colleges at Seventy-Five* (Washington: Association of American Colleges, 1988), p. 8.

6. Pfinster, "The American Liberal Arts College," p. 48.

7. Carnegie Foundation for the Advancement of Teaching, *A Classification of Institutions of Higher Education* (Princeton, 1987), pp. 3, 5. The drop in number of private colleges recorded in the Carnegie classification is a result primarily of reclassification of institutions rather than their failure; in most instances, colleges were moved into the category of comprehensive institutions.

8. National Federation of College and University Business Officers Associations, *The Sixty College Study: A Second Look* (Washington, 1960).

to a survey of operating data first collected between 1953 and 1954 from 60 private liberal arts colleges. The 1957–58 follow-up gave analysts an opportunity to examine trends in revenues and expenditures and to confirm that comparisons among colleges over time could be achieved and interpreted intelligibly. The authors concluded, on the basis of the follow-up, that such study can offer colleges a tool for administrative control, long-range planning, and fund-raising. In a comparison of trends over four years, the stability of the percentage allocations of funds to the various expenditure categories and the stability of revenue sources are the main findings. No sense of crisis or urgency permeates the report. The one concern expressed, however, pertains to the high outlays for student aid at one college in the Midwest:

> One rather alarming phenomenon appears among the "high" reports—a college in the Central Association diverting 15 percent of its educational and general income and 33.5 percent of its tuition income to student aid. This would suggest that the competition for students in the midwest is so strong that it is coming to be financed to a rather large extent by draining away resources that might otherwise bulwark the academic program.[9]

Words similar to these are spoken regularly today by college business officers, further evidence that worry about "over-spending" on student aid is a long-standing and perennial concern.

The post-World War II GI bill of rights, which Alice Rivlin called in 1961 "the most extensive venture into government aid for students in our history," was followed in 1958 by a second important piece of federal legislation, the National Defense Education Act.[10] This act, prompted by the Russian launch of *Sputnik* in 1957, included a national defense student loan program (NDSL),[11] national defense fellowships, and national defense language fellowships. The fellowship programs were aimed at doctoral education and thus did not provide support for students enrolled in liberal arts colleges, but the NDSL program was an important new source of financial aid available at the undergraduate level. When augmented by the programs created in the Higher Education Act of 1965 and the education amendments of 1972, students at

---

9. *The Sixty-College Study*, p. 25.

10. Alice M. Rivlin, *The Role of the Federal Government in Financing Higher Education* (Brookings, 1961), p. 64.

11. Subsequently renamed national direct student loans, and now Perkins loans, for former Senator Carl Perkins.

private colleges had an impressive array of federal grant, loan, and work-study programs on which to draw.

An event of far-reaching importance dating from this era was the development in economics of the "human capital" model of higher education as investment, analogous, metaphorically, to investment in physical capital. Theodore W. Schultz, of the University of Chicago, did early work on this concept, but it received its most complete treatment in the publication of Gary Becker's *Human Capital*.[12] This concept not only helped to justify student borrowing to finance higher education but contributed to the questioning of the size and scope of higher education's "public benefits." These benefits to the public were a rationale for heavily subsidized tuition levels through state support for public colleges and universities. In the ongoing debate over the proper share of college costs to be borne by students versus society, the human capital metaphor has weighed heavily on the side of those who argue that most benefits from college are private and captured by the student in the form of higher wages. This argument implies that the student, rather than society, should bear the larger share of costs, a position, incidentally, that is helpful to private colleges. The ramifications of the human capital concept are still being felt today in debates over how colleges and students should be financed.

The early and mid-1960s, years of exceptional growth in higher education, were also marked by a strong, noninflationary economy, capable of yielding annual productivity increases of 2 percent to 3 percent. Many students of higher education, including Hans Jenny and Richard Wynn, refer to this time as the golden years of American higher education. Their three publications traced the financial condition of 48 liberal arts colleges from 1960 to 1973 and were the first in a seemingly unending series of reports in the 1970s commenting on the financial plight of private education in general, and the liberal arts college in particular.[13] Discussion of curricular matters, central to work

---

12. Gary S. Becker, *Human Capital: A Theoretical and Empirical Analysis with Special Reference to Education*, 2d ed. (University of Chicago Press, 1980).

13. Hans H. Jenny and G. Richard Wynn, *The Golden Years: A Study of Income and Expenditure Growth and Distribution of 48 Private Four-Year Liberal Arts Colleges, 1960–68* (Wooster, Ohio: The College of Wooster, 1970); Hans H. Jenny and G. Richard Wynn, *The Turning Point: A Study of Income and Expenditure Growth and Distribution of 48 Private Four-Year Liberal Arts Colleges, 1960–70* (Wooster, Ohio: The College of Wooster, 1972); and G. Richard Wynn, *At the Crossroads: A Report on the Financial Condition of the Forty-Eight Liberal Arts Colleges Previously Studied in the Golden Years, The Turning Point* (University of Michigan, Center for the Study of Higher Education, 1974).

done in the late 1950s and 1960s, gave way to economics, as financial worries took center stage.[14]

In *At the Crossroads*, Wynn summarizes the findings of the first two reports as follows:

> When Hans Jenny and I titled our first study of these 48 colleges *The Golden Years*, we were referring to the generally prosperous early and mid-1960s. Enrollments grew slowly but steadily, a building boom was peaking, faculty and staff salaries were approaching desired levels, and peaceful campuses were the rule. The 48 colleges collectively finished each year with an operating surplus. But during the last several years of our study, ending in 1968, clearcut signs of financial distress became apparent, even for this sample of fairly well-to-do colleges.
>
> Our update to 1970 was *The Turning Point*, dramatizing how the addition of only two fiscal years brought an end to the golden years in a splash of red ink. Income was unable to keep pace with accelerating expenditure growth, particularly student aid. Enrollment dropped drastically in several institutions, benefactors proved fickle, and increasing price competition from public systems took its toll.[15]

In response to the budget deficits of the early 1970s, Wynn reported that the colleges had been able to reestablish balanced budgets, not by increasing revenues but by cutting expenditure growth. Rather than rejoice at this elimination of deficits, Wynn raises the specter of a new era in which "quality distress" replaces "financial distress" as the central problem. Colleges would survive, but survival would become the dominant concern, with innovation and improvements in quality sacrificed to the necessity of restraining growth of expenditures. Wynn ends the report with three scenarios: an optimistic one in which "public and private support reach new heights. Income again grows at increasing rates, and with it expenditures."[16] The pessimistic scenario shows revenues failing to grow, expenditures falling, quality declining, and colleges failing. The author's views, however, are found in the middle of these two extreme pictures. He sees financial stability being maintained, but "survival becom[ing] the crucial operating principle, as manifested in balanced budgets. Some institutions are able to

14. See Earl J. McGrath, ed., *Cooperative Long-Range Planning in Liberal Arts Colleges* (Columbia University, Teachers College, 1964); and Earl J. McGrath and Charles H. Russell, *Are Liberal Arts Colleges Becoming Professional Schools?* (Columbia University, Teachers College, 1958).

15. Wynn, *At the Crossroads*, pp. 2–3.

16. Wynn, *At the Crossroads*, p. 27.

maintain the quality of their program intact; for others, quality deterioration becomes the *modus vivendi.*"[17]

Meanwhile the principal federal policy affecting higher education during this period, the Higher Education Act of 1965, which had its origin in the Johnson administration's War on Poverty and the civil rights revolution, was broadening access to higher education. This landmark legislation established the educational opportunity grants program (the original version of the present supplemental educational opportunity grants [SEOG] program) and the guaranteed student loan program, both designed to help low- and middle-income students attend college. These programs exist to this day and are especially important to students in private colleges and universities.

The 1970s—New Problems, New Policies

While Jenny and Wynn were charting the changing fortunes of 48 private colleges, Earl F. Cheit, writing for the Carnegie Commission on Higher Education, brought national attention to the plight of all higher education in his 1971 publication, *The New Depression in Higher Education.*[18] The fundamental problem that Cheit and his colleagues documented was a tendency for costs to rise faster than income, producing a cost-income squeeze. A representative sample of 41 colleges and universities was studied, including 14 private liberal arts colleges. Based on that sample, Clark Kerr, chairman of the Carnegie Commission, in the foreword to the book projected that 29 percent of the nation's 730 liberal arts colleges were not in financial trouble, 43 percent were headed for trouble, and 28 percent were in financial difficulty.[19]

Interviews with presidents of the 14 private colleges produced the following picture, which could just as easily have been written in 1992 as twenty years earlier. "The financing of private education is in a crisis because of rising costs, fears that tuition has reached a 'saturation point,' desire to extend access to those who cannot afford it, decline in growth in the income which made up subsidies, and, finally, increased

17. Wynn, *At the Crossroads,* p. 28. Emphasis in original.
18. Earl F. Cheit, *The New Depression in Higher Education: A Study of Financial Conditions at 41 Colleges and Universities* (McGraw-Hill Book Company, 1971).
19. Cheit, *The New Depression,* p. x.

competition from state institutions."[20] Cheit concludes his analysis of
the financial problems facing private liberal arts colleges with the
following observation:

> In brief, administrators of the liberal arts colleges are struggling with
> the cost-income squeeze in a context that raises a larger issue. Their
> institutions offer an educational program that was once unique. Today,
> however, state institutions offer much the same program, often just as
> good qualitatively, and at much lower cost to the student. Not only does
> this pose a problem of financial competition, but it also raises the larger
> question of the role of the liberal arts college. Administrators of these
> institutions argue persuasively the case for diversity, for pluralism, and
> see the solution to their problem in gaining access to more federal and
> state funding while retaining their independence. They believe this should
> be done and can be done. For them the issue is when. The current
> financial squeeze adds urgency to this longer-range problem, for many
> of these institutions are getting into financial difficulty.[21]

A 1973 publication by William W. Jellema, *From Red to Black?*,
provided further information on the financial status of private colleges
and universities.[22] Based on data collected from 554 private institutions
during 1970 and 1971, the study documented growing financial pressures, including deficits in operating budgets similar to those highlighted
by Cheit. Among other things, the Jellema study emphasized the
growing burden of student financial aid provided by institutions from
their operating budgets:

> The increasing price difference [between public and private institutions]
> is a consequence of rapidly rising tuition in private higher education.
> This brings a further problem. As tuition increases, so must direct student
> aid; and since tuition is a major source of student aid funds, as student
> aid increases, so must tuition. This spiral is an outstanding reason for
> the deficit in the current accounts of many private institutions. At many
> of these colleges and universities, the difference between income and
> expenditures in the student aid account is precisely the deficit in the
> operating budget.[23]

As already noted, the relationship between tuition and student aid was
not a new issue twenty years ago. And today, it still bedevils private
colleges.

---

20. Cheit, *The New Depression*, p. 123.
21. Cheit, *The New Depression*, pp. 128–29.
22. William W. Jellema, *From Red to Black? The Financial Status of Private Colleges
and Universities* (Jossey-Bass Publishers, 1973).
23. Jellema, *From Red to Black*, p. xi.

At the federal level, enactment of the education amendments of 1972, one of the most far-reaching pieces of federal higher education legislation ever written, provided significant help in meeting the growing need for student financial aid. Among other provisions, this legislation established basic educational opportunity grants (now Pell grants) and state student incentive grants; reauthorized (with amendments) the college work-study program, guaranteed student loans, and national direct student loans; converted educational opportunity grants into supplemental educational opportunity grants; created the Student Loan Marketing Association, a government-sponsored private corporation, financed by private capital, to provide liquidity and facilitate transactions involving insured student loans; and established the National Commission on the Financing of Postsecondary Education.[24] This legislation created the basic pattern of federal student aid that remains to this day; there is no doubt that these programs of grants, loans, and work-study have played (and continue to play) a vital role in enhancing student access to higher education, as well as choice among institutions. Consequently, they contribute importantly to the survival of private colleges.

The remaining task in the 1970s was to focus attention on state policy and in particular to encourage states to introduce or expand tuition-offset grants. While such grants can take many forms, perhaps the most common is a need-based grant, provided from state funds, that an undergraduate student can use to cover some or all of tuition costs at a private college, usually within the student's state of residence. By providing a federal matching component, the newly enacted state student incentive grant (SSIG) program offered a financial incentive for state grants. A 1974 publication of the Association of American Colleges, *A National Policy for Private Higher Education*, strongly recommended the adoption or expansion of state student aid programs and helped to popularize the concept of tuition-offset grants.[25] According to the report, their purpose was to reduce or stabilize the

---

24. David W. Breneman and Chester E. Finn, Jr., eds., *Public Policy and Private Higher Education* (Brookings, 1978), pp. 453–54.

25. *A National Policy for Private Higher Education: The Report of a Task Force of the National Council of Independent Colleges and Universities* (Washington: Association of American Colleges, 1974). The Carnegie Council also endorsed these forms of aid; see Carnegie Council on Policy Studies in Higher Education, *The States and Private Higher Education: Problems and Policies in a New Era* (San Francisco: Jossey-Bass Publishers, 1977).

public-private tuition gap, thought to be the central economic problem of many private colleges. The states responded with varying generosity to these arguments, and by 1976, thirty-nine states had one or more such programs, including, in nearly every instance, a need-based grant scheme.[26]

The early 1970s witnessed an outpouring of national reports on the financing of higher education, prepared by such groups as the Carnegie Commission, the Committee for Economic Development, and the National Commission on the Financing of Postsecondary Education.[27] These reports were responding in large measure to the growing role that the federal government seemed destined to play in helping students pay for college, through grants, loans, and work study. The problems of financing private higher education were touched on in these reports, largely through support for direct financial aid to students, thereby encouraging student choice. This was a time of considerable intellectual ferment, as policy analysts and others attempted to merge the new federal programs into a system that had previously relied on state and private support of institutions.

By the mid-1970s the basic financial structure that operates to this day was in place. Although the federal student aid programs are reauthorized and modified every few years, changes still function within the framework established by the education amendments of 1972. As a consequence, the studies published in the last half of the 1970s, for the most part, either gave advice to administrators, forecast trends, or supplied data on current developments. For example, the Carnegie Foundation published *More Than Survival* in 1975, reporting on "prospects for higher education in a period of uncertainty." This volume included a review of past growth in higher education, enrollment projections to the year 2000, forecasts for institutions, and suggestions on what administrators could do. It closed with a short chapter on public policy.[28]

26. Breneman and Finn, *Public Policy*, p. 47.

27. Carnegie Commission on Higher Education, *Higher Education: Who Pays? Who Benefits? Who Should Pay?* (McGraw-Hill Book Company, 1973); Committee for Economic Development, *The Management and Financing of Colleges* (New York: CED, 1973); and National Commission on the Financing of Postsecondary Education, *Financing Postsecondary Education in the United States* (Washington, 1973).

28. Carnegie Foundation for the Advancement of Teaching, *More Than Survival: Prospects for Higher Education in a Period of Uncertainty* (San Francisco: Jossey-Bass Publishers, 1975).

In the same year, Howard Bowen and John Minter published the first of four annual reports on financial and educational trends in private higher education.[29] Supported by a grant from the Lilly Endowment, these reports drew on survey data collected from a stratified sample of 100 private colleges and universities. The annual reports were designed to monitor the progress of private colleges and universities and provide timely data on financial and educational trends for administrators and policymakers. Once again, we see an activity designed for purposes other than the advocacy of new programs or policies. The 1978 report did, however, note the dramatic, growing importance of federal student aid and its favorable effect on the "financial progress of the institutions."[30]

The Breneman-Finn volume on private higher education, published by Brookings in 1978, was an exception to this trend.[31] This book advanced the radical thesis that the financing of higher education would be more efficient and more equitable if state subsidies were concentrated on need-based student aid, portable over state lines, rather than on direct appropriations for institutions. Anticipating a decade or more of enrollment decline, the authors urged a marketlike system that would allow student choice to determine which colleges and universities survived and which declined. It called for a sharp increase in the federal state student incentive grant program (SSIG) that, with its matching provisions, would supply a strong incentive for state governments to shift aid away from institutions and into student aid. The hostile political reaction to this proposal from representatives of public higher education doomed it politically at that time.[32]

Finally, the Carnegie Council on Policy Studies, at the end of more than a decade of concentrated study of higher education by the Carnegie Commission and Carnegie Council, published *Three Thousand Futures*, informing readers that each college and university would determine its

29. Howard R. Bowen and W. John Minter, *Private Higher Education* (Washington: Association of American Colleges, 1975). The 1976 and 1977 reports had the same title and publisher, while the 1978 report was entitled *Independent Higher Education,* and was published by the newly created National Association of Independent Colleges and Universities (NAICU).

30. W. John Minter and Howard R. Bowen, *Independent Higher Education* (Washington: NAICU, 1978), p. 73.

31. Breneman and Finn, *Public Policy.*

32. The federal policy advocated in the Breneman-Finn volume is currently under serious discussion at the state level, for example, in Minnesota and Pennsylvania.

own future, that some would thrive and others falter, and that intelligent and informed choices would be essential to success.[33] On this note, the 1980s began.

The 1980s—A Decade of Surprises

What most observers thought the 1980s would be like can be read directly from the titles of books and monographs published in the late 1970s and early 1980s: *Surviving the Eighties*; *The Enrollment Crisis: Factors, Actors, and Impacts*; *Challenges of Retrenchment*; *The Three "Rs" of the Eighties: Reduction, Reallocation, and Retrenchment*; and *The Coming Enrollment Crisis: What Every Trustee Must Know*. The analyses were based on demographic facts and extrapolations of economic trends. It was widely assumed that a 25 percent drop in the 18-year-old population, beginning in 1979 and lasting into the mid-1990s, would produce a decline in undergraduate enrollments of between 5 and 15 percent (although some extreme projections were made on both up and down sides). By 1980 the poor performance of the U.S. economy in the 1970s had produced double-digit inflation and high unemployment (known as stagflation), rapidly rising energy costs, a standstill in productivity growth, and declining real incomes.[34] Furthermore, the mainline economics profession had few clear remedies to propose; the economy defied the logic of the Keynesian system that had guided policy in the post-World War II years. Another concern unique to higher education was the decline in the economic rate of return to higher education, publicized by Richard B. Freeman in a widely read 1976 volume, *The Over-Educated American*.[35] In short, no wonder most observers expected the 1980s to be a time of decline for much of higher education, with a clear focus on retrenchment and survival. More than one analyst shared Robert Behn's view of liberal arts colleges, expressed in congressional testimony. He said that as many

33. Carnegie Council on Policy Studies in Higher Education, *Three Thousand Futures: The Next Twenty Years for Higher Education* (San Francisco: Jossey-Bass Publishers, 1980).

34. For an excellent discussion of these trends, see Frank Levy, *Dollars and Dreams: The Changing American Income Distribution* (W.W. Norton & Company, 1988).

35. Richard B. Freeman, *The Over-Educated American* (Academic Press, 1976).

as 200 of these small, tuition-dependent institutions would fail during the 1980s.[36]

That reality turned out to be so different from the projections has to be attributed primarily to the upsurge in the economy (including income redistribution that favored high-income families), and secondarily to responses and adaptations of colleges and universities.[37] History's final judgment on the wisdom of Reagan economic policies is not yet in, but a sharp recession triggered by tight monetary policy in the early 1980s broke the back of inflation, and expansionary fiscal policies and supply-side incentives helped to produce one of the longest periods of unbroken growth in modern times. Although the federal budget slid into steadily deeper deficits, most state governments experienced sharp revenue growth, a positive element for higher education. A redistribution of income toward the wealthy enhanced the fund-raising potential of both private and public colleges and universities.[38] In the final analysis, the well-being of higher education is so closely tied to the well-being of the economy that planners can virtually ignore other conditions; the only problem is that no one can accurately forecast the economy.

Other surprises in the 1980s affected higher education. Largely because the bottom fell out of the job market for high school graduates, the economic return to a college education reversed itself, with the wage premium for college graduates increasing between 1979 and 1986 to levels larger than those found in any earlier period.[39] As a result, the college-going rate of high school graduates between the ages of 18 and 24 reversed its decline of the 1970s (when it hit a low of 29.7 percent in 1973), reaching 34.0 percent in 1986.[40] A combination of higher college-going rates and continued growth in the enrollment of

36. Robert D. Behn, "The End of the Growth Era in Higher Education," statement presented to the Committee on Labor and Human Resources, United States Senate, Duke University, Institute of Policy Sciences and Public Affairs, 1979.

37. See Kevin Phillips, *The Politics of Rich and Poor: Wealth and the American Electorate in the Reagan Aftermath* (Random House, 1990).

38. Phillips, *The Politics of Rich and Poor.*

39. Kevin Murphy and Finis Welch, "Wage Premiums for College Graduates: Recent Growth and Possible Explanations," *Educational Researcher*, vol. 18 (May 1989), pp. 17–26.

40. National Center for Education Statistics, *Digest of Education Statistics 1989* (Department of Education, 1989), p. 199.

older and part-time students kept total enrollments stable, rather than declining over the decade.[41]

The revenues of most colleges also took an unanticipated jump during the 1980s. Between 1981 and 1989, tuition in private institutions increased by an unprecedented 106 percent in nominal terms, far outstripping the growth in incomes.[42] After a decade or more of research that stressed the critical need to reduce, or at least stabilize, the tuition gap between public and private institutions, with tuition increases in private colleges kept to a minimum, the actual experience was a stunning reversal. Contrary to what might have been expected, students were not driven away by these rapidly rising prices, and at many institutions, particularly the more selective ones, applications went up. Some observers speculated that parents and students were seeking quality more fervently than in previous years, and were, to some extent, judging quality by price.[43] Some presidents of private colleges saw little incentive to keep prices down, particularly if that had the effect of lowering the institution's actual or perceived quality.[44]

This change in pricing behavior reflected another striking change in the 1980s, the growing tendency of college administrators to focus on marketing and strategic planning.[45] Presidents, admissions officers, business officers, and development staff focused intensely on the institution's niche in the market for higher education services and how it was positioned in comparison with competitors. Admissions officials conducted survey research on student applicants, including not only those who were admitted and did not enroll but also those who did not complete the formal application process. Business officers followed tuition levels closely to ensure that the college's price accurately reflected its place in the academic pecking order. The worst sin was

41. Between 1980 and 1987, total head-count enrollment increased from 12.1 million to 12.8 million. *Digest of Education Statistics 1989*, p. 167.

42. College Board, "Trends in Student Aid: 1980 to 1989," New York, College Board Publications, August 1989, p. 11.

43. For an enlightening discussion of such behavior, see Tibor Scitovsky, "Competition in the Uninformed Market," in *Welfare and Competition: The Economics of Fully Employed Economy* (Chicago: Richard D. Irwin, 1951), chap. 18, pp. 398–413.

44. The author, while serving as president of a private college during this time, engaged in many such conversations with other presidents.

45. This tendency was given a strong push by a widely read book written by George Keller, *Academic Strategy: The Management Revolution in American Higher Education* (Johns Hopkins University Press, 1983).

to underprice a college relative to schools deemed weaker. Development staff spent untold hours on public relations activities, striving to bring the college's name forward in those communities where both students and dollars were sought. Although much maligned by presidents, the annual reports on *America's Best Colleges*, published by *U.S. News and World Report*, popularized the pecking order and gave it third-party validity in the public mind.[46]

These changes instilled in college leaders a marketing mentality much more pronounced than had existed in earlier times. Ideas about pricing behavior were taken from the business sector of the economy. It was observed, for example, that in the retailing business, department stores were moving toward one of two poles; those that stressed low price through heavy discounting and offered limited service, and those that stressed quality and service and played down price. Stores caught in the middle not clearly serving one market or the other were the ones most often hurt. The lesson for most private colleges was not to get caught in the middle trying to keep prices down, but rather to emphasize quality and service in the belief that a strong demand existed for such services. Whether this approach was a sound long-range strategy for many private colleges is debatable, but this type of thinking contributed to the willingness to raise tuitions by double-digit amounts year after year in the 1980s.

Another surprise was the explosive growth of the stock market throughout much of the decade, achieving an unprecedented annual rate of gain of 17.4 percent.[47] The result for most colleges was a sharp increase in the market value of endowments, which translates into increased revenue for operating budgets.[48] The booming stock market also helped fund-raising activities, both annual giving and capital campaigns. Many small colleges did not have a history of sophisticated fund-raising activities before the 1980s, but most advanced far along the learning curve during that decade, launching campaigns and devel-

46. The editors of *U.S. News and World Report*, *America's Best Colleges and Professional Schools*, an exclusive survey, Washington, 1990 (and previous annual editions).

47. Data are for the Standard and Poor's 500-stock index. See Karen Slater, "The '80s: The Decade Investors Cashed In Despite the Crash and Other Traumas," *Wall Street Journal*, December 15, 1989, p. C1.

48. Most colleges follow the total return method of spending, generally based on a fixed percentage of a multiyear moving average of the value of the endowment.

oping the necessary volunteer support organizations required for success. These efforts produced another increased flow of revenues for most colleges.

It is more difficult to generalize about trends in federal and state support for students attending private colleges.[49] Federal grant programs did not increase as rapidly as college costs, thus falling in real value. Loan volume grew sharply, however, providing students with access to capital at subsidized rates. State student aid programs also grew in most states, although often starting from low levels. Relative to expectations, state and federal programs were disappointing to many college leaders; nonetheless, they often provided the margin of difference that allowed a student to attend a private college.

In short, the chief revenue sources of most private colleges—tuition (determined by price and enrollment), endowment earnings, annual giving, fund drives—moved in the same direction during the 1980s—up.[50] If one thinks of these revenues as a portfolio, a more normal pattern over a decade might be gains in some areas, losses in others. Interestingly, in the 1980s each revenue source for most colleges went in a positive direction (despite earlier forecasts). It seems unlikely that this trend will continue during the 1990s.

No 1980s policy studies or significant legislative actions have been mentioned, and that reflects accurately the intellectual vacuity of this unusual decade. At the federal level, the emphasis shifted to attacks on higher education, elevated to a high art by William Bennett, President Reagan's secretary of education.[51] The criticisms were financial and ideological—colleges and universities were criticized for their sharp tuition increases and runaway costs, but also, as noted in chapter 1, for moving away from the canon of Western European thought.[52] The policy process in Washington degenerated into budget warfare, largely devoid of thought, with the Reagan administration proposing dramatic

49. For a good summary, see College Board, "Trends in Student Aid: 1980 to 1989."

50. Chapter 4 in this volume presents financial data supporting this point, showing the variation among colleges on these measures.

51. See, for example, Secretary Bennett's speech at Harvard University's 350th anniversary, reprinted in *American Higher Education: Purposes, Problems and Public Perception* (Queenstown, Md.: Aspen Institute, 1992), pp. 187–99.

52. Sharp tuition increases, and the growing public outcry about them, no doubt contributed to the decision of the Department of Justice to launch in 1989 an unprecedented antitrust investigation of the pricing and related policies of more than 50 colleges and universities.

cuts in federal student aid programs, while college lobbyists concentrated their efforts to save programs on Congress. The growing federal budget deficit also threw a damper on creative thought, as it became clear that little, if any, new money would be forthcoming. The Carnegie Commission on Higher Education and the Carnegie Council on Policy Studies, which had done so much to enrich the discussion of higher education policy in the late 1960s and 1970s, were gone, and private foundation support for such efforts largely shifted to studies of elementary-secondary education, where a crisis of quality was widely perceived to exist.

With thought and action at the federal level diminished, attention turned to the states but with little result. At the decade's end, Frederick Fischer, a budget examiner with responsibility for student aid programs at the Office of Management and Budget, wrote a plaintive article in which he bemoaned the absence of serious discussion of new forms of state financing for higher education:

> As we have seen, rationales for the low-tuition policy began to break down in the 1960s, as large numbers of poor students found the non-tuition threshold too great an obstacle to higher education. It is not too surprising, then, that significant levels of public discussion about the matter date from that period, with the greatest amount of interesting writing in the late 1960s and early 1970s. What is surprising is that this discussion lasted only a decade, culminating for all practical purposes in 1978 with chapters on state financing by Robert Berdahl and Colin Blaydon in *Public Policy and Private Higher Education*, edited by David Breneman and Chester Finn.
>
> What happened? Why did all the voices fall silent? Why isn't anyone talking about state financing of higher education any more?[53]

Fischer suggests several explanations for this lack of thought, but the central point of his article is accurate. After a decade of silence, the recession of the past three years has reopened these issues in new and lively ways.

53. Frederick J. Fischer, "State Financing of Higher Education: A New Look at an Old Problem," *Change,* vol. 22 (January–February 1990), p. 49.

CHAPTER THREE

Enrollment, Tuition, and Financial Aid

THE SHARP increase in student aid provided by the institution itself, often referred to as unfunded student aid, or as institutionally provided student aid, is among the most troubling economic problems confronting liberal arts colleges. It is not unusual to find a college currently devoting 20 percent or more of its budget to unfunded student aid, at the same time that outlays on instruction constitute no more than 40 percent of the budget. One can understand why presidents worry when, for every dollar spent on instruction, fifty cents goes for student aid. Business officers often prepare a financial analysis that tracks the percentage allocation of the budget to various expenditure categories over time, and the rapidly rising share of unfunded student aid over the past decade is causing many college presidents and business officers to lose sleep at night.

I believe that this critical area of college finance is not well understood on many campuses, and that the analyses typically done may help to produce faulty decisions. Indeed understanding the complicated interaction of tuition, enrollment, composition of the student body (quality and diversity), and financial aid is central to the financial welfare of private colleges. The following economic theory of the behavior of private colleges helps to explain that interaction.

A Microeconomic Theory of the Private College

The theory draws on the work of David Hopkins and William Massy, presented in *Planning Models for Colleges and Universities*.[1] In that

1. David S. P. Hopkins and William F. Massy, *Planning Models for Colleges and Universities* (Stanford University Press, 1981), pp. 73–130.

volume, they develop a general theory of the behavior of nonprofit institutions and then specify the model to represent a research university. I have modified their general model to fit my understanding of the behavior of a private college.

Hopkins and Massy argue that university administrators seek to maximize a value function that ranges over variables defining university activities, stocks, and prices. Activities include flow variables such as enrolled student-years, employed faculty-years, additions to library holdings, and so forth. Inputs and outputs of the educational and research efforts of the university are included. Stocks include the physical plant, endowment, and related physical and financial resources. Prices include the array of tuition charges, salaries, and reductions in tuition that are awarded in unfunded student aid. The value function covering these variables is increased as much as possible, subject to several constraints: a production function constraint, embodying educational values and technology; supply and demand constraints for inputs (for example, faculty) and for students; and the budget constraint that requires total revenue to equal total cost.

Hopkins and Massy argue that optimization occurs in two stages. In the first stage, basic educational patterns are laid down, as academic deans and faculty establish the organization and nature of the curriculum, number and size of classes, student-faculty ratios, and so forth. In this fashion, the educational production function is determined, although no one would be so crude as to refer to it by that name. Relationships, such as the student-faculty ratio, are chosen to meet the budget constraint. Supply and demand constraints are also incorporated into this first stage. In the second stage, administrators seek to increase qualitative aspects of the value function, for example, quality of research or of teaching, also subject to the budget constraint.

In the spirit of their approach, I suggest that the first-stage optimization for the private college means setting the desired enrollment, as well as creating the inputs (faculty, staff, facilities, and so forth) needed to serve that enrollment at a financially sustainable quality. My experience, borne out by the site visits conducted for this book, teaches that every college has a desired enrollment that it seeks to maintain, usually within some fairly narrow range. The numbers can be put together in a simple example as follows: the college seeks to offer twenty majors, with an average of four faculty for each major, and with a student-faculty ratio of 15:1. These educational decisions yield a desired faculty size of 80 and a student body of 1,200. The number and distribution of faculty will permit general education courses and the desired majors, and the college will build and maintain a physical plant and related facilities (library, laboratories, dormitories) to accommodate an enrollment of this size. Most colleges seek stability in these basic relationships, not wanting enrollment or faculty numbers to fluctuate much from year to year. Occasionally a college will decide to expand enrollment, but such a change is usually a one-time event, and stability is sought at the new level, with appropriate adjustments to faculty size and physical plant. Decisions that make up the first-stage optimization are made on a long-term basis, not annually.

In the second stage, the college seeks to increase the quality of its student body, faculty, and facilities as much as possible, given the decisions about size made in the first stage, and subject to budget constraints. The determinants of total revenue are an essential part of that budget constraint, and net tuition revenue (gross tuition revenue minus unfunded student aid) is, for most colleges, the largest single revenue source.[2] No wonder administrators worry about the rapid growth of unfunded student aid, which would seem to reduce net tuition revenue (for all but the most selective colleges, unfunded student aid is simply a tuition discount, awarded to an admitted student as a scholarship).[3]

One economic distinction among colleges influences the interpretation of unfunded student aid in the following analyses. A subset of the colleges in this sector can be highly selective in admissions because they enjoy very large applicant pools. These highly selective colleges could, if they chose, fill their entering classes entirely with students able to pay the full tuition price, rendering unfunded student aid unnecessary. Most private colleges, however, must literally discount tuition on a selective basis to meet their enrollment goals. If the highly selective colleges were interested solely in obtaining the greatest tuition revenue possible, they would abandon the policy of need-blind admissions (admitting students without reference to family income, and

2. Colleges differ in the decision to dedicate unrestricted gifts to student financial aid, which causes the measure of unfunded student aid to be understated for some colleges.

3. See William G. Bowen and David W. Breneman, "Student Aid: Price Discount or Educational Investment?" *Brookings Review*, vol. 11 (Winter 1993), pp. 28–31, for a discussion of times when student aid is, and is not, properly viewed as a tuition discount.

meeting the resulting financial need), and simply fill their entering classes with students from high-income families. These colleges do not behave in this fashion because their educational values commit them to invest in a more diverse and higher-quality student body than they would achieve without any institutionally provided student aid. Their relative wealth and attractiveness as educational institutions permit them to follow a policy of need-blind admissions, and the tuition reductions they award to low-income students are a true expense because a full-pay student has been denied in order to enroll a scholarship student. William Bowen and I have described this situation elsewhere as one in which highly selective colleges use unfunded student aid, not as a tuition discount to meet the school's enrollment target, but as an educational investment in the quality and diversity of the student body.[4]

If all private colleges were in this fortunate position, there would be little need for a book on the future of liberal arts colleges. Most colleges in this sector, however, must admit a high percentage of applicants and must use tuition discounting to meet their enrollment goals.[5] The challenge, therefore, is to understand how most private colleges, apart from the highly selective few, make intelligent decisions about tuition, student aid, and enrollments. The economic model developed here applies to most private colleges, where tuition discounting is a necessary operating practice.[6]

It is hypothesized that the college seeks to maximize the quality and diversity of its student body and the quality of faculty and facilities, while meeting desired goals for enrollment, faculty, and related educational resources. To achieve these objectives, the college incurs operating and capital costs, which must be covered by total revenues. Tuition is the most important source of revenue for most colleges, and thus the tuition rate is a key decision variable that the college sets annually.

The variables can be defined as follows:

$$\text{let } X_N = \text{ desired enrollment, for example,}$$
$$1,150 \le X_N \le 1,250$$
$$X^* = \text{ desired educational resources for } X_N$$

4. Bowen and Breneman, "Student Aid."

5. National data cited in chapter 1 document the high levels of financial need found among students enrolled in the private sector, indicating that private colleges cannot achieve their enrollment goals with full-pay students.

6. See appendix C for a formal presentation of the model.

P = tuition rate

X_Q = student quality or diversity

X_Q^* = quality of educational resources

TR = total revenue

TC = total cost

The college is assumed to have completed its first-stage maximization, during which the desired levels of enrollment, X_N, and of educational resources (faculty, facilities, library holdings, laboratories, and so on), X^*, have been chosen. It is also operating with a tuition rate, P, chosen to be consistent with the resource mix embodied in X^*, and to be in line with its peer group of competitors. At the second stage, the college seeks to enhance the quality of its students, faculty, and facilities, X_Q and X_Q^*, assuming that the desired enrollment, X_N, and the desired level of educational resources, X^*, have been achieved. In seeking to enhance quality, the college must meet the budget constraint, $TR - TC \geq 0$.

The next step is to focus on the elements that determine total revenues and total costs to understand how the budget constraint influences the decisionmaking of administrators who seek to meet the college's goals. Because tuition is the dominant revenue source for most private colleges, the linkage among the published tuition price, unfunded student aid, and enrollments is the central financial puzzle that must be solved if the financing of these colleges is to be understood.

Figure 3-1 depicts a selective college going through each step in the standard admissions process—applications, acceptances, and final enrollment. In this hypothetical example, D1 represents application demand, with students ranked by ability to pay if accepted. D2 represents demand by all applicants who meet minimal acceptance requirements; in this step, the college may reject some full-pay students in favor of higher-quality applicants with lower family incomes. D3 is the final demand that results when all accepted students have decided where to attend; more full-pay students are lost, and the college has been forced to dip farther down in the income distribution to meet the enrollment target and to accept students for quality and diversity. In this example, the college is seen to play an active role in selecting and enrolling the "optimal" class. Had the college chosen to accept all of the full-pay applicants, and if they had enrolled, unfunded student aid would be minimized.

Figure 3-1. *Steps in the Admissions Process at a Selective College*

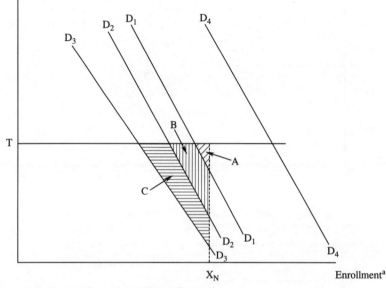

D₁D₁   Demand by all applicants who would attend if accepted.

D₂D₂   Demand by all applicants who meet minimum academic criteria (that is, who could graduate) and who would attend if accepted.

D₃D₃   Demand by entering class admitted and matriculating.

Special case:
D₄D₄   Demand at small number of institutions that could fill class with qualified students who would pay full tuition.

Unfunded aid:
         = A if no qualification is used for admission.
         = A + B if minimum criteria are used.
         = A + B + C if admission process seeks "optimal" characteristics of student body.

a. Enrollments generated at below nominal tuition can reflect the use of either need-based or merit scholarships.

Of course, the college does not know in advance how many full-pay applicants will accept an offer of admission, nor how many of the aided applicants will enroll. What a college does know from experience is roughly how many full-pay applicants are likely to enroll, and thus how many students will require varying amounts of financial aid. Figure 3-2 presents the final demand pattern facing a representative college, assuming that it has done all that it can to increase applications and acceptances.

Figure 3-2. *Enrollment Demand and Unfunded Student Aid*

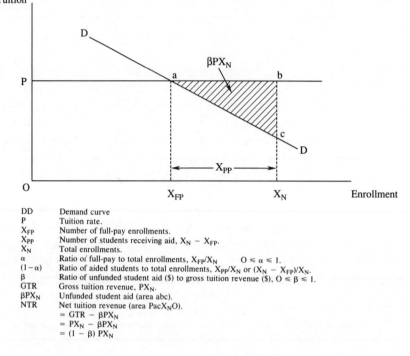

DD	Demand curve
P	Tuition rate.
X_{FP}	Number of full-pay enrollments.
X_{PP}	Number of students receiving aid, $X_N - X_{FP}$.
X_N	Total enrollments.
α	Ratio of full-pay to total enrollments, X_{FP}/X_N $0 \leq \alpha \leq 1$.
$(1-\alpha)$	Ratio of aided students to total enrollments, X_{PP}/X_N or $(X_N - X_{FP})/X_N$.
β	Ratio of unfunded student aid (\$) to gross tuition revenue (\$), $0 \leq \beta \leq 1$.
GTR	Gross tuition revenue, PX_N.
βPX_N	Unfunded student aid (area abc).
NTR	Net tuition revenue (area $PacX_NO$).
	$= GTR - \beta PX_N$
	$= PX_N - \beta PX_N$
	$= (1 - \beta) PX_N$

Figure 3-2 depicts a downward-sloping demand curve (DD) that, in some form, faces each college at the end of each recruiting year.[7] In particular, I am assuming that colleges are able to operate, to varying degrees, as price-discriminating monopolists.[8] The monopolistic element enters in through the ability of each college to distinguish itself as a unique enterprise, offering an educational experience different

7. The demand curve simply depicts the relationship between the college's tuition and the number of students able and willing to pay it. When tuition discounts are introduced, the quantity demanded increases, as additional students are able to pay the lower net price. A college can plot these relationships from historic data; the only part not accessible is the section of the curve above the tuition price. That section can be approximated by tracking changes in full-pay applicants from year to year as tuition increases, although a possible shift in the demand curve from one year to the next muddies the analysis.

8. This concept is explained in any introductory text on microeconomics. For an interesting application in the field of medicine, see Reuben A. Kessel, "Price Discrimination in Medicine," Journal of Law and Economics, vol. 1 (October 1958), pp. 20–53.

from that found elsewhere. Although liberal arts colleges have many similarities, each differs from its peers by some combination of location, history, religious affiliation, single-sex or racial orientation, curricular emphasis, and perceived quality (or prestige). To varying degrees, these features give each college a downward sloping demand curve, as opposed to a market in which each seller faces a single price. Indeed, the colleges included in this study had tuition prices in 1991 that ranged from $19,905 to $3,338, with a mean of $10,784, and standard deviation of $3,238.[9] Although higher education is a very competitive enterprise in many respects, it is not an industry in which competition produces a common price.[10]

The price-discriminating element in the model enters in through financial aid, which effectively allows the college to charge different prices to different students, based on financial need or merit. In any college with an enrollment of, say, 1,200 students, many different prices are being paid—one group receives no aid and pays the published tuition price, while students receiving financial aid pay prices based on individual financial circumstances. Though such a pricing scheme can be portrayed as socially beneficial, the fact remains that the college is able to price differentially along the demand curve, capturing for itself much of the "consumer surplus" that would have gone to students and parents had there been a single, competitively determined, lower price.[11]

Figure 3-2 highlights the essential features of this analysis. The figure assumes that enrolled students have been ranked on the basis of ability to pay, with the full-pays generating enrollment up to X_{FP}, while those on financial aid cover enrollment from X_{FP} to X_N.[12] Two parameters are highlighted: alpha, α, the ratio of full-pay to total

9. Author's calculations based on data from the College Board.

10. Prices for colleges of comparable quality are, of course, much closer together than the range of all private college prices.

11. The actual market-clearing price (the price that would eliminate excess demand without any financial aid) would vary dramatically among colleges depending on the number and wealth of applicants and the relative attractiveness of the college. Market-clearing tuition rates for an Amherst or Williams could easily be higher than their current rates, but most colleges in this study would find the market-clearing rate lower than their current tuition. In figure 3-2, the market-clearing price would be the vertical distance $X_N c$.

12. This final enrollment distribution is the result of earlier decisions, in which students of varying financial capacity apply, are accepted, and enroll. At each of these earlier stages, a similar financial ranking can be made.

enrollments, and beta, β, the ratio of unfunded student aid to gross tuition revenue. In the financial accounts of colleges, gross tuition revenue is defined as the published tuition price times total enrollment, without reference to the financial aid awarded. This treatment of tuition revenue is a peculiarity of the accounting system used in higher education and is a potential source of confusion in the analysis of financial aid. Colleges report gross tuition revenue, defined as above, on the revenue side of the ledger, while unfunded student aid is entered as an expense on the debit side of the ledger. In figure 3-2, gross tuition revenue is the area determined by PX_N, while unfunded student aid is the area $a\ b\ c$, which is equal to βPX_N. The accounting is misleading because it paints a picture of a college able to earn the full amount of gross tuition revenue, while treating unfunded student aid as a discretionary variable. As figure 3-2 shows, this view is mistaken, for the demand curve determines the number of students able or willing to pay the full tuition price, with financial aid (discounts) used to reach the desired enrollment level. In the absence of those discounts, the college would enroll fewer students.[13]

Figure 3-2 also displays the financially meaningful tuition variable, net tuition revenue, which is the revenue that the college actually receives from students and the various external sources of funds.[14] Net tuition revenue is simply gross tuition revenue minus unfunded student aid, area $P\ a\ c\ X_N\ O$ in figure 3-2, or $(1 - \beta)PX_N$ algebraically. Net tuition revenue is the figure that colleges should be tracking, rather than unfunded student aid (not a fully discretionary variable), or the ratio of unfunded student aid to educational and general expense, which suggests a level of control not available to the less selective colleges.

Simple inspection of figure 3-2 suggests that if a college were interested in maximizing net tuition revenue, it would set tuition at the level where the demand curve intersects the vertical axis, enrolling just one full-pay student and discounting down the demand curve until

13. As noted earlier, highly selective colleges with large applicant pools are the one exception to this conclusion, for they could reach their desired enrollment goal with full-pay students. For this small group of colleges, unfunded student aid is used exclusively to enhance the quality and diversity of the student body, not simply to meet an enrollment goal.

14. For the purpose of defining net tuition revenue, endowed student aid owned by the college is treated as an external source of revenue, analogous to Pell grants, guaranteed student loans, and parental payments. In the long run, however, colleges can increase endowed student aid, thereby reducing reliance on unfunded aid, all else equal.

the desired enrollment level is reached. In this fashion, the college could in principle extract all of the consumer surplus from students and their families. It is reasonable to ask, then, why colleges do not set tuition in this fashion. On reflection, one sees several brakes on such behavior. First, all colleges would have to raise prices together for such a response to be possible for any one college; a single college that unilaterally raised tuition dramatically would suffer a sharp loss of applications. The demand curve for each college will be highly elastic in the region above current tuition. Second, it is already difficult for colleges to convey to students and parents that the posted tuition price is not necessarily the net price that a student will pay after eligibility for financial aid is determined. A sharp increase in tuition, therefore, would be expected to produce "sticker shock" and cause applications to fall. The potential to increase net tuition revenue by raising tuition sharply is only effective if total enrollments are not diminished, but constant enrollments in this case can hardly be assumed. Third, any college that raised tuition abruptly would be subject to an outpouring of critical commentary, and few, if any, colleges would be willing to face such criticism alone.

Nonetheless, while the above arguments explain the absence of unilateral actions to raise tuition sharply, the logic of figure 3-2 demonstrates a clear financial incentive for increasing tuition, if other colleges raise their prices at comparable rates.[15] I believe an implicit understanding of this situation contributed to the sharply escalating tuition rates of the 1980s.

With a bit of algebraic manipulation (see appendix C), the relationships in figure 3-2 yield another way of viewing the variable β. It can be shown that β (the proportion of gross tuition revenue devoted to unfunded student aid) equals the proportion of enrolled students receiving aid, times the average discount per aided student. This relationship means that the value of β increases as the percentage of students on aid goes up and as the size of the average award increases.[16]

15. The situation is complicated by the presence of state universities with highly subsidized tuition; increased tuition in the private sector relative to the public might simply result in enrollments shifting into the public sector, rendering many private colleges losers.

16. As should be evident from the earlier discussion of figure 3-2, as well as the above discussion, an increase in β does not mean a decrease in net tuition revenue as long as enrollment is stable; for reasonable changes in the values of P, $\overline{P}$ (average tuition paid by students receiving aid), and α, both β and net tuition revenue increase. See table 3-6.

In the demand curve facing the hypothetical college in figure 3-2, one sees that the college can set the desired enrollment, X_N, the level of educational resources, X^*, and the tuition rate, P, but that these decisions, coupled with the demand curve facing the college, will determine the financially important values of α, $\overline{P}$, and β, where $\overline{P}$ is defined as the average tuition paid by students receiving unfunded student aid. The amount of unfunded student aid is determined by the demand curve interacting with decisions on the desired enrollment and the tuition rate.

The above conclusion is subject to two qualifications. First, as noted earlier, a small number of highly selective colleges could fill their entering classes with full-pay students if the schools chose to increase their net tuition revenue. That these colleges do not make that choice shows that they are willing to incur a real cost (an opportunity cost) in turning away full-pay students to enroll others who require financial aid. These colleges are seeking to optimize the quality and diversity of students enrolled, X_Q, and are bearing a real cost in doing so. For these few colleges, the ratio of unfunded student aid to total educational expenditures is a meaningful measure of the cost to achieve greater quality and diversity.

Second, even less selective colleges, which make up most schools in this sector, do exercise some selectivity in admissions, presumably turning down some full-pay students. The ability to exercise some selectivity is a form of organizational flexibility (or slack), and its presence gives a college the capacity to modify admissions policies, if necessary, in search of greater net tuition revenue.[17] For example, if a college suffers a drop in applications or enrollments, it can change admissions standards to favor higher-income students to make up lost tuition revenue. In the extreme, a college may come under such severe financial pressure that its ability to exercise any selectivity will be eliminated, and the college will, in essence, be forced to operate as if it were a profit-making firm.[18]

In summary, net tuition revenue—not gross tuition revenue—is the financially meaningful measure that most colleges should be tracking:

17. Larry Leslie, University of Arizona, has noted the intricate trade-offs among net tuition revenue, student quality, and student diversity that a college must consider in its admissions decisions.

18. Hopkins and Massy, *Planning Models*, p. 107.

—When a less selective college specifies a desired enrollment and tuition rate, it loses much of its control over the amount of unfunded student aid that will be required to meet those goals. Alternatively, if a college seeks to set a limit on unfunded student aid, the consequence will be reduced control over the level or quality of enrollments. If a college is unable to be selective (the extreme case), then limiting unfunded student aid will result in declining enrollments. Each college will find itself located on the continuum somewhere between limited control over the enrollment level or limited control over the amount of unfunded student aid.

—The commonly computed ratio of unfunded student aid to educational and general expenses is, for all but the most selective colleges, a number with limited meaning, for it implies a level of control not present.

—The ratio of unfunded student aid to gross tuition revenue is a more meaningful number because it is directly related to the demand curve facing the college.

—The analysis also highlights the importance of the percentage of full-pays enrolled and the size of the average discount. The notion that tuition increases may "price a college out of the market" can be interpreted directly from this definition of β; increases in price are likely to reduce the percentage of full-pays enrolled and raise the size of the average discount. Increases in the value of β, however, do not imply a necessary drop in net tuition revenue, as data presented later demonstrate. For net tuition revenue to decline, enrollments must fall or the demand curve must shift down and to the left, sharply reducing the number of full-pay students and raising the average discount. Each college would be advised to examine its recent experience, analyzing for several years the impact of changes in the values of β, α, and $\overline{P}$ on net tuition revenue. The result will be a better understanding of the college's demand curve and its market niche, which is essential if the college is to increase control over the level of net tuition revenue.

To complete this development of an economic theory of the private college, the revenue and cost functions that make up the budget constraint must be examined. Total revenue is the sum of net tuition revenue, earnings on endowment, and other revenues, such as annual giving. Total costs are essentially fixed in the short run, equal to the sum spent on the mix of resources required to serve the desired enrollment level. (Remember that the desired enrollment is treated as the midpoint of a range, for example, 1,200 as the desired level, 1,150 to 1,250 as the range.) Each college will have its enrollment range determined by the first-stage optimization of the dean and faculty, which in turn determines the desired input levels, X^*, for that size. In the short run, that is, an academic year, the marginal cost of enrollment shifts within that range is minimal; the faculty and facilities are fixed for the contract period, and all that happens is a modest change in the average class size. This logic, coupled with the implicit understanding of the demand curve facing a college, prompts colleges (rationally) to discount tuition to the point that enrollment falls within the desired range. With the marginal cost effectively zero, any gain in net tuition revenue leaves the college in a stronger financial position for that year.

If the college operates outside the desired range, short-run marginal costs may rise or fall as a function of enrollments. Even within an academic year, enrollments that exceed the range may force the college to hire part-time instructors to cover additional sections, while enrollments that fall below the range may force the college to lay off part-time instructors. In an academic year, however, other financial adjustments are usually possible.

The most common response to an unexpected enrollment shortfall is to increase the pay-out rate on endowment. In essence, the college dips for one year into quasi endowment, funds that trustees have transferred to endowment but which can be spent if necessary. (In the long run, of course, colleges seek to increase their endowments to reduce dependence on tuition and thus vulnerability to unexpected declines in enrollment.) An increase in the pay-out rate on endowment moves the college out of financial equilibrium, however, and if the likelihood of increasing net tuition revenue is low, the college may have to explore the economic and educational consequences of a smaller operating size.

Net tuition revenue can be increased in several ways, singly or in combination, as follows:

—Efforts can be directed to shift the demand curve up and to the right, allowing the college to attract more full-pay students. The sharp increase in outlays for recruiting in recent years—more expensive viewbooks, videotapes promoting the college, visits to more high schools, trips to the college for high school counselors—are attempts to shift the demand curve and alter its shape. Public relations efforts are equally important, for the rankings a college receives in publications such as the *U.S. News and World Report*'s annual issue on college quality can have a noticeable impact on the number and quality of applicants.

—Unless enrollment falls, tuition increases will result in higher net tuition revenue, even if the amount of unfunded student aid also increases, absorbing some of the gain. It is not possible to give a simple rule for tuition increases that will apply to all colleges; instead, officials at each college must develop an understanding of the demand curve that the college faces, including the elasticity of response to increases in tuition. Figure 3-2 shows that an increase in price, with the demand curve unchanged, results in fewer full-pay students and more unfunded aid; the important issue, however, is the change in net tuition revenue, which in turn depends upon the elasticity of demand.

—A college can alter admissions standards to enroll some students based on ability to pay full tuition. When one of the highly selective colleges announces, with some embarrassment, that it is being forced to discontinue need-blind admissions, it is opting for this policy. In the extreme, a college may lose all of its ability to be selective, with no alternative but to admit students based on ability to pay. Changing admissions policy is not without its risks, however, for it may produce a negative feedback from potential applicants in future years.

Importantly, capping the amount of unfunded student aid is not an option in this group of potential policies. And yet, that is precisely the type of move that college officials are tempted to try, ignoring the logic of the downward sloping demand curve. Capping unfunded student aid at some arbitrary percentage of the expense budget, unrelated to the demand curve, could result in lower enrollments and a loss in net tuition revenue. Furthermore, college officials who become preoccupied with limiting the growth of unfunded aid fail to see that it is but one part of a larger, more complex mosaic, and not an independent variable. Because unfunded student aid appears in the accounting ledger as an expense, however, officials are tempted to treat it as a discretionary item that does not affect other parts of the operating statement. Fortunately, the inherent logic of comparing marginal revenue to marginal cost is understood by most college officials, and a decision to cap the aid budget is usually overridden as the reality of the admissions picture and the amount of financial need becomes clear. Rather than arguing about the amount of unfunded student aid to budget each year, college officials would be advised to spend more time analyzing the changes in net tuition revenue that a combination of marketing, student aid, and tuition increases can generate. The context of budget discussions on many campuses would improve if sterile debates about the amount of unfunded student aid were replaced by an emphasis on the nature of demand for the college and the role that student aid can play as part of an operating strategy to increase net tuition revenue and its role in enhancing the quality and diversity of the student body.

If a college has exhausted all efforts to increase net tuition revenue, as well as other sources of financial support, while continuing to run an operating deficit, then administrators must determine whether a new financial equilibrium can be found with lower enrollment and costs. If officials can significantly reduce costs without jeopardizing academic vitality, then enrollments may be reduced with a minimal loss in net tuition revenue by denying admission to students with high financial need. (Such a policy may violate the values of faculty, students, alumni, administrators, and trustees, and be difficult to accept; unfortunately, the alternative may be closure.) Many of the colleges in this study, however, are already so small that downsizing may not be a realistic possibility for them. In that case, barring outside intervention, closure may be necessary; that decision, hard as it is, may be preferable to a situation in which the college ceases to perform a valuable function or operates ineffectively because it has become too small.

Finally, even if a college is operating with a balanced budget, and with the desired enrollment, costs will rise from year to year.[19] To meet the budget constraint, revenue must also rise by a like amount. Increases in tuition are one obvious, and necessary, way to meet cost increases. Consistent with the theory advanced in this chapter, analysis of tuition increases should focus on changes in net tuition revenue. If costs increase by 10 percent, then net tuition revenue must also rise by that amount, assuming all other revenue sources rise by the same proportion. If demand will not allow that much increase in net tuition

19. The reasons (and justifications) for cost increases are not my focus here; discussions of that topic can be found in Arthur M. Hauptman with Jamie P. Merisotis, *The College Tuition Spiral: An Examination of Why Charges Are Increasing* (Macmillan Publishing Company, 1990), and Michael S. McPherson and Morton Owen Schapiro, *Keeping College Affordable: Government and Educational Opportunity* (Brookings, 1991).

Table 3-1. *Applications, Acceptances, and Enrollments for 138 Colleges, Selected Years, 1977–91*

Item	1977	1983	1988	1989	1990	1991
Applications	162,564	185,662	222,853	241,792	234,869	221,652
Acceptances	102,038	111,854	123,127	127,603	129,906	131,530
Enrollments	48,643	47,219	49,129	50,033	48,724	46,421
Selectivity[a] (%)	62.8	60.3	55.3	52.8	55.3	59.3
Yield[b] (%)	47.7	42.2	39.9	39.2	37.5	35.3
Enrollment of applicants[c] (%)	29.9	25.4	22.0	20.7	20.7	20.9
Average applicants per college	1,178	1,345	1,614	1,752	1,702	1,606
Average acceptances per college	739	810	892	924	941	953
Average enrollment per college	352	342	356	363	353	336

Source: Author's calculations based on data from the College Board, New York. See appendix A.
a. Percent of applicants accepted.
b. Percent of accepted students who enroll.
c. Percent of applicants who enroll.

revenue, then other revenue sources must rise disproportionately, or costs must be reduced. If neither option is possible, then the college will be in permanent financial disequilibrium and may be forced to close, merge, or become a publicly supported institution.

Applications, Acceptances, and Enrollments

To gain insight into the demand facing liberal arts colleges, I requested data from the College Board on the number of students who applied, were accepted, and enrolled in the 212 colleges in this study. Table 3-1 presents these data for the 138 colleges that reported figures to the College Board consistently for the years 1977, 1983, 1988, 1989, 1990, and 1991. For these colleges, applications increased sharply between 1977 and 1989 (49 percent) but declined by 8 percent between 1989 and 1991. Acceptances increased steadily over the years covered, while entering enrollments fluctuated modestly around a mean of 48,360 (figure 3-3).

Selectivity, the ratio of acceptances to applications, increased from 63 percent admitted in 1977 to 53 percent in 1989 but moved back to 59 percent admitted in 1991.[20] Yield, the percentage of accepted students who enroll, declined steadily from 48 percent in 1977 to 35

20. Defined in this way, selectivity increases as the ratio decreases, that is, as the percentage of applicants who are admitted declines.

Figure 3-3. *Application, Acceptance, and Enrollment Data for 138 Liberal Arts Colleges, Selected Years, 1977–91*

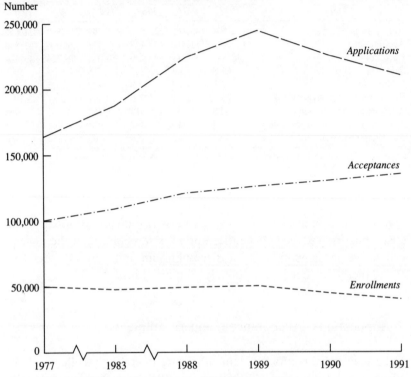

Number

Source: Author's calculations based on data from the College Board, New York.

percent in 1991. A third ratio, enrollments to applications, has no shorthand name and is difficult to interpret unambiguously, that is, it is not clear whether a decline in the ratio represents a positive or negative change.[21] It could be viewed as a workload measure that reveals how many applicants are required to enroll one student. Viewed in this way, the data show that one hundred applicants generated thirty enrollments in 1977 but only twenty-one in 1991.

How does one evaluate the data in table 3-1? Which trends are positive, and which are worrisome? The growth in applicants between 1977 and 1989 is probably positive unless there has been a steady increase in the number of students who submit multiple applications.

21. In this ratio, the intervening effect of the college's admissions decisions is absent, which helps to explain the ambiguity.

The 49 percent increase in applications may mask what is actually a much smaller increase in potential students if, as some admissions officials believe, students in the 1980s applied to more schools than did their counterparts a decade earlier. That applications increased during most of the 1980s, when the number of high school graduates dropped by about 10 percent, is a tribute to the extensive recruiting efforts mounted by these colleges.[22] Dire forecasts of enrollment decline in the 1980s changed admissions offices from gatekeepers to aggressive recruiters.

A potentially troubling feature of the data in table 3-1 is the steady decline in yield, implying that these colleges collectively were less attractive, for whatever reason, to admitted students at the end of the period than at the beginning.[23] This trend also means that more students have to be recruited and admitted each year to maintain level enrollments. (In 1977, 102,000 acceptances produced 48,600 enrollments, while in 1991, 131,500 acceptances produced only 46,400 enrollments.) These figures help to explain why the cost of each enrolled student has increased steadily over the years.

The data in table 3-1 also bear directly on the economic theory of private colleges presented earlier. The number of students enrolled each year is essentially stable; when applications rose sharply, colleges increased their selectivity rather than expand. In recent years, when applications fell, selectivity declined to maintain enrollments. Both observations are consistent with the theory, which assumes that colleges seek to enhance the quality and diversity of students while maintaining a desired enrollment. Changing selectivity is the adjustment factor that keeps enrollments and quality as high as possible, given shifts in the number of applications and in the yield rate.

Table 3-2 presents data for these colleges for selected years, with the figures broken down by groupings in decending order of financial and enrollment strength (see appendix A). Because a high percentage of colleges in the weakest four deciles did not report data to the College Board, the numbers in those groups were too small to report; consequently, in table 3-2, groups 7–10 have been combined into a

22. National Center for Education Statistics, *Digest of Education Statistics 1990* (Department of Education, 1991), p. 109.

23. If the number of applications per student did increase during these years, then that fact alone would lower the yield rate, which would be a less troubling explanation for a declining yield rate.

Table 3-2. *Applications, Acceptances, and Enrollment, by College Group, Selected Years, 1977–91*

Year and group[a]	Average applicants per college	Average acceptances per college	Average enrollment per college	Selectivity (%)	Yield (%)	Enrollment of applicants (%)
1977						
1	2,722	1,056	461	38.8	43.6	16.9
2	1,765	1,081	451	61.2	41.7	25.6
3	1,161	857	400	73.8	46.6	34.4
4	1,040	797	374	76.6	46.9	36.0
5	799	632	293	79.1	46.4	36.4
6	690	581	311	84.2	53.5	45.0
7–10	591	490	279	82.9	57.0	47.3
Total	1,178	739	352	62.7	47.7	29.9
1983						
1	3,014	1,172	468	38.9	39.9	15.5
2	2,083	1,197	451	57.5	37.7	21.7
3	1,459	961	387	65.9	40.2	26.5
4	1,252	880	356	70.3	40.5	28.4
5	880	675	273	76.7	40.5	31.1
6	733	600	282	81.9	47.1	38.5
7–10	636	531	269	83.5	50.6	42.2
Total	1,345	810	342	60.2	42.2	25.4
1988						
1	3,679	1,282	474	34.8	37.0	12.9
2	2,503	1,267	458	50.6	36.2	18.3
3	1,765	1,055	397	59.8	37.6	22.5
4	1,515	1,029	392	67.9	38.1	25.9
5	1,062	733	305	69.0	41.6	28.8
6	870	676	306	77.7	45.3	35.2
7–10	735	592	277	80.5	46.8	37.7
Total	1,614	892	356	55.3	39.9	22.1
1991						
1	3,406	1,351	470	39.7	34.8	13.8
2	2,333	1,373	436	58.9	31.8	18.7
3	1,751	1,110	367	63.4	33.0	20.9
4	1,686	1,158	361	68.7	31.2	21.4
5	1,022	768	266	75.1	34.6	26.0
6	887	649	258	73.2	39.8	29.1
7–10	850	636	271	74.8	42.6	31.9
Total	1,606	953	336	59.3	35.3	20.9

Source: See table 3-1.

a. Groups are arranged in descending order of financial and enrollment strength. See appendix A, especially table A-2, for individual college rankings.

single grouping. Several findings are what one would have predicted; the average number of applications is higher in the stronger schools and declines steadily down the deciles. The average size of entering class also tends to be larger in the stronger groups, but here the relationship is not monotonic. Not surprisingly, selectivity also decreases as the groups descend, although the differences among the bottom half of the spectrum (groups 5 to 10) are small and do not always follow the declining pattern.[24] Even the least selective colleges commonly reject between 15 percent and 25 percent of their applicants, indicating that some selectivity is to be found in virtually all of these colleges.

Somewhat surprising is that yield tends, if anything, to increase as one moves from the stronger to weaker groups of colleges. In all four of the years included in table 3-2 groups 7–10 have the highest yield, while groups 1 and 2 generally have the lowest yields. One can suggest reasons for these trends after the fact, that is, greater competition among top colleges for a more national student body, less competition among the more regional schools, but I do not think that these results were obvious a priori. Similarly, the ratio of enrollments to applications is lower in the more selective colleges than in the less selective ones.

Seventeen of the 24 women's colleges reported to the College Board in each of the six years, and the trends for these colleges are presented in table 3-3. In general, the pattern is similar to that of all colleges in the data set, but the changes are less dramatic. While applications for all colleges were up 49 percent between 1977 and 1989, they increased by only 21 percent for the women's colleges. Entering enrollments were generally stable until 1991, when they dropped 8 percent from the prior year. Selectivity was essentially unchanged at about 60 percent accepted, and yield declined from 50 to 41 percent.

Unfortunately, virtually none of the historically black colleges reported to the College Board for these six years, so no data for them can be presented. There are, however, data for 19 Presbyterian, 17 Methodist, and 9 Roman Catholic colleges, reported in table 3-4.[25] Again, the pattern does not deviate significantly from that of all colleges, although the timing of changes for the Catholic colleges is different

24. Selectivity was one of three measures used to define the groups.
25. These three denominations have the largest number of colleges affiliated with them—see appendix A for full information.

Table 3-3. *Applications, Acceptances, and Enrollments, Seventeen Women's Colleges, Selected Years, 1977–91*

Item	1977	1983	1988	1989	1990	1991
Applications	14,918	16,752	16,477	18,032	17,815	17,247
Acceptances	9,802	9,702	9,761	10,220	10,184	10,303
Enrollments	4,866	4,652	4,591	4,663	4,583	4,231
Selectivity (%)	65.7	57.9	59.2	56.7	57.2	59.7
Yield (%)	49.6	47.9	47.0	45.6	45.0	41.1
Enrollment of applicants (%)	32.6	27.8	27.9	25.9	25.7	24.5
Average applicants per college	878	985	969	1,061	1,048	1,015
Average acceptances per college	577	571	574	601	599	606
Average enrollment per college	286	274	270	274	270	249

Source: See table 3-1.

from the rest. Applications for Catholic colleges dropped in 1988 compared with 1983 but then increased steadily between 1988 and 1991. Selectivity has remained reasonably stable for all three groups of religiously affiliated colleges, while yield has declined for all three, in roughly the same way for all colleges in the data set. As with women's colleges, these data do not suggest that Presbyterian, Methodist, or Catholic colleges are experiencing application or enrollment trends that differ significantly from the experience of all colleges.

Net Tuition Revenue and Unfunded Student Aid

Table 3-5 shows the tuition revenue and unfunded student aid by the ten strength groups for two recent years, fiscal 1988 and 1989.[26]

Of particular interest in table 3-5 are the values for β, the ratio of unfunded student aid to gross tuition revenue. That figure can be computed directly from national surveys by dividing unfunded student aid by gross tuition revenue. However, β cannot be computed from the more interesting and alternative formula discussed in appendix C, for the surveys do not collect data on the number of full-pay students. Each campus has that information about itself and thus can calculate for its own case all of the variables in figure 3-2.

26. See appendix A for a discussion of data sources.

Table 3-4. *Applications, Acceptances, and Enrollments
for Religiously Affiliated Colleges, Selected Years, 1977–91*

Item	1977	1983	1988	1989	1990	1991
Applications						
Presbyterian	15,354	18,060	23,778	25,534	24,074	22,565
Methodist	14,816	17,228	19,761	22,201	21,772	19,972
Catholic	8,505	9,358	8,881	9,649	9,788	9,832
Acceptances						
Presbyterian	10,823	11,904	14,448	14,878	14,758	14,965
Methodist	12,357	13,461	15,145	16,474	16,116	15,504
Catholic	4,985	5,692	4,633	5,120	5,514	5,987
Enrollments						
Presbyterian	5,335	5,182	5,704	5,778	5,695	5,671
Methodist	6,009	5,535	5,809	6,042	5,743	5,181
Catholic	2,706	2,693	2,077	2,265	2,232	2,249
Selectivity (%)						
Presbyterian	70.5	65.9	60.8	58.3	61.3	66.3
Methodist	83.4	78.1	76.6	74.2	74.0	77.6
Catholic	58.6	60.8	52.2	53.1	56.3	60.9
Yield (%)						
Presbyterian	49.3	43.5	39.5	38.8	38.6	37.9
Methodist	48.6	41.1	38.4	36.7	35.6	33.4
Catholic	54.3	47.3	44.8	44.2	40.5	37.6
Enrollment of applicants (%)						
Presbyterian	34.7	28.7	24.0	22.6	23.7	25.1
Methodist	40.6	32.1	29.4	27.2	26.4	25.9
Catholic	31.8	28.8	23.4	23.5	22.8	22.9
Average applicants per college						
Presbyterian	808	951	1,251	1,344	1,267	1,188
Methodist	872	1,013	1,162	1,306	1,281	1,175
Catholic	945	1,040	1,110	1,206	1,224	1,229
Average acceptances per college						
Presbyterian	570	627	760	783	777	788
Methodist	727	792	891	969	948	912
Catholic	554	632	579	640	689	748
Average enrollment per college						
Presbyterian	281	273	300	304	300	298
Methodist	353	326	342	355	338	305
Catholic	301	299	260	283	279	281

Source: See table 3-1.

Table 3-5. *Average Gross and Net Tuition Revenue, Student Aid, and β, by College Group, 1988, 1989*[a]

Constant 1989 dollars except for β

Item	1988	1989	Item	1988	1989
All groups			*Group six*		
Gross tuition	8,147	8,767	Gross tutition	7,037	7,553
Net tuition	6,715	7,208	Net tuition	5,921	6,282
Student aid	1,432	1,559	Student aid	1,116	1,271
β	18	18	β	16	17
Group one			*Group seven*		
Gross tuition	12,004	13,067	Gross tutition	6,445	7,026
Net tuition	10,408	11,361	Net tuition	5,227	5,711
Student aid	1,596	1,706	Student aid	1,218	1,315
β	13	13	β	19	19
Group two			*Group eight*		
Gross tuition	10,746	11,724	Gross tutition	6,455	6,834
Net tuition	9,100	9,738	Net tuition	5,253	5,578
Student aid	1,646	1,986	Student aid	1,202	1,256
β	15	17	β	19	18
Group three			*Group nine*		
Gross tuition	9,852	10,634	Gross tutition	6,238	6,664
Net tuition	8,295	9,022	Net tuition	5,028	5,381
Student aid	1,557	1,612	Student aid	1,210	1,283
β	16	15	β	19	19
Group four			*Group ten*		
Gross tuition	8,966	9,704	Gross tutition	5,009	5,347
Net tuition	7,202	7,784	Net tuition	3,946	4,151
Student aid	1,764	1,920	Student aid	1,063	1,196
β	20	20	β	21	22
Group five					
Gross tuition	8,325	8,933			
Net tuition	6,444	6,914			
Student aid	1,881	2,019			
β	23	23			

Source: Author's calculations based on data from the National Center for Education Statistics. See appendix A.
a. Tuition and aid calculated per full-time-equivalent (FTE) student; beta expressed in percent.

Table 3-5 shows that gross and net tuition revenue per FTE decline dramatically as the groupings descend, with net tuition revenue in 1989 in group 10 only 37 percent of that in group 1.[27] The values of β, however, are much closer, ranging from a low of 13 percent in group 1 to a high of 23 percent in group 5. The average value of β for all groups, 18 percent, was unchanged from 1988 to 1989—years in which college officials bemoaned the rapid growth of unfunded student aid. Such aid was certainly increasing, but so were gross and net tuition revenue, with the result that the relationships among them in 1988 and 1989 were essentially unchanged.

Interestingly, values for β peak in group 5, suggesting that colleges in the middle of the pack may face certain types of recruiting difficulty not encountered in the most prestigious, or least prestigious, colleges. The explanation, which is necessarily speculative, may be that middle-tier colleges are caught in an uncomfortable marketing position in comparison with the higher-priced but clearly more prestigious top colleges and the considerably lower-priced, least prestigious colleges. Perhaps middle-tier colleges carry a tuition price that many students and families perceive as too high for the quality, or prestige, provided by these schools, with the result that these colleges are forced into heavier discounting than those at either end of the spectrum. These concerns prompted my opposition to sharp tuition increases during the 1980s when I served as president of a group 5 college.[28] I feared that middle-tier colleges were being swept along by the leadership of the top colleges into prices that would cause growing numbers of families to question the value of our academic degrees relative to their cost. Increased reliance on so-called merit aid in recent years by colleges below the top tier might be explained as a response to these pressures.

The counterargument, however, is that the strategy of raising tuition and increasing discounts has produced gains in net tuition revenue

27. Again, one would expect these values to decline down the groups because net tuition revenue per FTE student was one of the measures used in ranking the colleges. The amount of difference in revenue, however, attributable in part to the much lower tuition rates found in the lower-ranked colleges, is notable.

28. Jean Evangelauf, "President Says 100 Private Colleges Follow Crowd: The Higher Their Prices, the More Students Apply," *Chronicle of Higher Education*, March 2, 1988, p. A29; and David W. Breneman, "Time for Honesty: The Truth about College Tuition," *Change*, vol. 22 (January–February 1990), p. 9.

for colleges in every strength grouping, as the figures in table 3-5 demonstrate. While group 1 increased net tuition revenue by 9 percent between 1988 and 1989, group 5 had a 7 percent increase, not as good certainly, but still a substantial gain. On the one hand, the relative position of colleges in the middle tiers of prestige may mean that they will experience more price resistance than the top colleges from potential full-pay students as tuitions increase; that is, the middle-tier colleges face a more elastic demand curve and thus must discount more often. On the other hand, the demand curve shifts each year and is sufficiently inelastic that, even with greater discounting, they still realize substantial gains in net tuition revenue from year to year (figure 3-2). In light of these conflicting forces, it is not clear where wisdom lies. As long as a college realizes gains in net tuition revenue, it is hard on narrow economic grounds to criticize its pricing and student aid policies.[29] The danger, however, is that continued increases in tuition of 8 to 10 percent a year may eventually reduce the number of full-pay students to such a low level for some colleges that further increases in net tuition revenue may be foreclosed. Obviously, it is helpful if peer institutions increase their tuitions at roughly the same rate.

Table 3-6 reports values of β and net tuition revenue per FTE student for 1978, 1983, and 1989. The values of β clearly increased, from 11 percent in 1978 for all colleges in the data set, to 13 percent in 1983, and to 18 percent in 1989. Furthermore, values of β for each of the ten groups also increased (or remained stable in a few cases) over this period, except for the drop from 17 percent to 15 percent between 1978 and 1983 for group 8. As noted earlier, an increase in β does not mean that net tuition revenue falls; in fact, just the opposite occurred, as table 3-6 shows. We computed values for net tuition revenue per FTE student for all colleges and by the ten groups for 1978, 1983, and 1989, and used the consumer price index to convert the earlier two years to 1989 dollars. In every case, the colleges experienced substantial gains in net tuition revenue in real terms, despite the increased values of β. As the theory suggests, and these

29. On a broader economic view, however, college pricing policies that undermine trust may be very damaging. See the stimulating article by Gordon C. Winston, "Hostility, Maximization, and the Public Trust," *Change*, vol. 24 (July–August 1992), pp. 20–27.

Table 3-6. *Value of β and Average Net Tuition Revenue, by College Group, Selected Years, 1978–89*
Constant 1989 dollars except for β

College group	Value of β (%)			Average net tuition revenue per FTE student		
	1978	1983	1989	1978	1983	1989
All groups	11	13	18	5,153	5,629	7,189
One	8	11	13	7,536	8,738	11,358
Two	9	12	17	6,718	7,516	9,741
Three	9	12	15	6,436	7,097	9,022
Four	10	13	20	5,587	6,082	7,783
Five	12	18	23	5,499	5,830	6,914
Six	11	13	17	4,495	4,978	6,282
Seven	13	13	19	4,032	4,577	5,711
Eight	17	15	19	4,155	4,565	5,578
Nine	12	14	19	4,474	4,550	5,381
Ten	14	14	22	3,351	3,722	4,151

Sources: National Center for Education Statistics. See appendix A; and *Economic Report of the President, February 1991*, p. 351.

data confirm, the negative effect on operating statements of increased tuition discounting in recent years has been exaggerated.

Table 3-7 contains comparable data on tuition revenue and unfunded student aid for five additional groups—women's colleges, historically black colleges, and Presbyterian, Methodist, and Roman Catholic colleges. One is struck once again by the stability from one year to the next in the values of β; the only change is the drop from 17 percent to 16 percent for the women's colleges. Two groups—historically black colleges and Catholic colleges–have relatively low values for β; black colleges also have sharply lower levels of gross and net tuition revenue than in the sector at large or in any other group examined. The black colleges display a financial pattern that one would expect in a group of schools that enrolls predominantly low-income students. In that situation, there is little point in having a high tuition price that virtually no one pays, coupled with tuition discounts for all. These colleges have obviously adopted the sensible policy for their schools of low tuition and low unfunded aid, relying on external sources of funds, such as Pell grants, for the lowest-income students.

Table 3-7. *Gross and Net Tuition Revenue, Unfunded Student Aid, and β, by Type of College, 1988, 1989*[a]

Constant 1989 dollars except for β

Item	1988	1989
Women's colleges		
Gross tuition	8,208	8,728
Net tuition	6,911	7,371
Student aid	1,297	1,357
β	17	16
Black colleges		
Gross tuition	3,644	4,171
Net tuition	3,202	3,692
Student aid	442	479
β	12	11
Presbyterian colleges		
Gross tuition	7,544	8,158
Net tuition	5,855	6,336
Student aid	1,689	1,822
β	22	22
Methodist colleges		
Gross tuition	6,742	7,284
Net tuition	5,488	5,928
Student aid	1,254	1,356
β	19	19
Catholic colleges		
Gross tuition	6,512	7,172
Net tuition	5,643	6,227
Student aid	869	945
β	13	13

Source: Author's calculations based on data from the National Center for Education Statistics. See appendix A.
a. Tuition and aid calculated per FTE student; beta expressed in percent.

The financial pattern in historically black colleges differs radically from other colleges, while the pattern in women's colleges is strikingly similar to that of the total sector (figure 3-4). These differences will be discussed later when the site visits to 12 colleges are described.

Net Tuition Revenue and Expenditures

The final analyses in this chapter focus on the questions; Are increases in net tuition revenue keeping pace with increases in educa-

Figure 3-4. *Average Gross and Net Tuition Revenue and Student Aid, Women's Colleges and Black Colleges, 1989*[a]

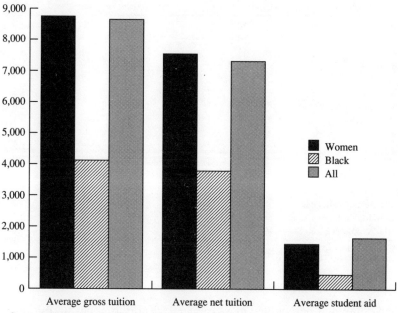

Tuition

Average gross tuition   Average net tuition   Average student aid

Legend: Women / Black / All

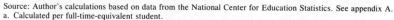

Source: Author's calculations based on data from the National Center for Education Statistics. See appendix A.
a. Calculated per full-time-equivalent student.

tional and general expenses? Has tuition discounting reached such a level that colleges are not able to match percentage increases in costs with comparable increases in net tuition revenue? To answer these questions, one must look at changes in expenses and in net tuition revenue.

I began with 190 colleges with usable data for fiscal 1988 and 1989, the two most recent years available. To compare annual changes in net tuition revenue and educational and general expenditures, I subtracted unfunded student aid from both sides of the ledger. (That it is necessary to subtract unfunded student aid from the expense side, as well as the revenue side, simply illustrates again the misleading nature of the accounting framework. For all but the most selective institutions, tuition not received—unfunded student aid—should not be viewed as an outlay comparable to salaries and book purchases.) I

Table 3-8. *Percent Increase in Expenditures, Net Tuition Revenue, and All Revenue, by College Group, Fiscal 1988–89*[a]

Group or type of college	Expenditure	Net tuition revenue	All revenue
All	10.2	11.3	10.9
One	10.0	10.2	9.0
Two	11.9	9.4	8.4
Three	10.7	11.0	11.8
Four	12.9	11.9	11.6
Five	10.6	12.4	11.1
Six	9.0	9.9	12.0
Seven	8.6	11.5	10.7
Eight	9.8	11.6	11.7
Nine	10.7	12.7	11.2
Ten	8.2	12.5	11.6
Women's colleges	11.0	11.0	11.0
Black colleges	9.5	11.3	14.3
Presbyterian colleges	12.1	12.6	9.7
Methodist colleges	12.5	11.9	12.7
Catholic colleges	10.5	10.8	9.6

Source: See table 3-7.
a. Calculated per FTE student.

then computed percentage increases in expenditures, net tuition revenue, and all revenues between 1988 and 1989.[30]

For the 178 colleges shown in table 3-8, expenditures increased by 10.2 percent between 1988 and 1989, while net tuition revenue went up by 11.3 percent, and all revenues by 10.9 percent, clearly covering the increased outlays.[31] The same pattern held for most of the ten groups, except for groups 1, 2, and 4. In group 1, net tuition revenues matched the increase in outlays, but all revenues fell short by a modest

30. All revenues include tuition and fees; federal grants and contracts; private gifts, grants, and contracts; and endowment income. We included this broader category because changes in total revenues—not just in net tuition—relative to costs ultimately determine the financial well-being of a college.

31. Twelve colleges reported data that seem implausible, that is, expenditures or revenues that declined more than 20 percent, or increased more than 30 percent, in one year. I assumed that these figures represented a change in reporting procedure or were simply in error and thus excluded them from the data reported in table 3-8. The colleges excluded were Pomona, Mt. Holyoke, Randoph-Macon Woman's College, Agnes Scott, Coe, Wells, Concordia (Mich.), Morehouse, Blackburn, Greensboro, Neumann, and Judson (Ala.). HEGIS and IPEDS data are a source of difficulty because of their incompleteness, but they are all that is available on a national basis.

amount. In groups 2 and 4, the gain in net tuition revenue fell short of the increase in costs, although only in group 2 is the shortfall relatively large (11.9 versus 9.4 percent). Interestingly, the lower-ranked groups covered their increased expenses comfortably with gains in both net tuition revenue and all revenue. A one-year change hardly tells the complete story, of course, and one should track these numbers annually. It is certainly possible that financial distress will arise in the 1990s.

Table 3-8 also includes similar data for 18 women's colleges, 8 historically black colleges, 22 Presbyterian, 22 Methodist, and 16 Catholic institutions. Revenue increases equaled or exceeded expenditure gains between fiscal 1988 and 1989 in the women's and historically black colleges, two groups thought by some to be in relative financial difficulty. The Methodist colleges also covered cost increases with revenue gains, but the Presbyterian and Catholic colleges were not as fortunate. These two groups increased net tuition revenue by more than expenditures, but they lagged in revenue from all sources. Data such as the above need to be tracked annually to determine the presence or absence of financial distress.

CHAPTER FOUR

Trends in Revenue and Expenditure

IN THIS chapter the focus on the financial activity of liberal arts colleges broadens from the relationship between tuition and student aid to the entire operating statement, encompassing revenues and expenditures. Examining changes over time in the sources and uses of funds will shed more light on the financial circumstances of these colleges.

One important, fundamental change, however, has been made in the standard accounting format used by colleges. Consistent with the discussion in chapter 3, in the tables in chapter 4, unfunded student aid provided by the colleges has been subtracted from both the revenue and expenditure sides of the budget, on the ground that it is best seen as forgone institutional revenue rather than spending on educational programs.[1] Tuition revenue, therefore, is expressed net of financial aid, which is not included on the expense side of the ledger.[2] Data on student aid are presented as separate entries in the tables but not as part of educational and general (E&G) expenditures.[3]

1. For further discussion of this issue, see William G. Bowen and David W. Breneman, "Student Aid: Price Discount or Educational Investment?" *Brookings Review*, vol. 11 (Winter 1993), pp. 28–31.

2. Endowed student aid is excluded from this measure of net tuition revenue. For those colleges that have moved unrestricted funds into the endowment as financial aid, my figures will understate the share of institutional funds going into student financial aid.

3. This same method is followed in Scott W. Blasdell, Michael S. McPherson, and Morton Owen Schapiro, "Trends in Revenues and Expenditures in U.S. Higher Education: Where Does the Money Come From? Where Does it Go?" DP-17, Williams Project on the Economics of Higher Education, Williams College, June 1992.

Change during Three Decades

For institutions whose origins date back one hundred years or more, comparative study of college financial accounts is a fairly recent activity. The first effort at a systematic comparison of revenues and expenditures among liberal arts colleges occurred in the early 1950s. "In 1954 an experiment unique in the history of higher education in America was undertaken by a group of sixty colleges. Prosaically, this experiment was, on the surface, nothing more exciting than an orderly gathering together, for purposes of comparison, of the details of income and expenditures in the participating colleges for the fiscal year 1953–54."[4] The initial effort in 1954 demonstrated that comparable data could be collected from the colleges, and a follow-up study took place four years later. The 56 colleges that participated in 1958 are a subset of those included in this study; therefore, financial data for fiscal 1958 and 1989 for these colleges can be compared to examine changes in the sources and uses of funds over the thirty-one-year interval (tables 4-1 and 4-2).[5]

The income figures shown in table 4-1 are striking for the minimal change recorded between 1958 and 1989; the shares represented by endowment, gifts and grants, and tuition declined modestly, while government support grew from a negligible base to nearly 7 percent of average revenues. Nonetheless, the overall pattern is one of stability, with tuition playing the dominant role. Expenditure, however, shows significant change in several categories. The sharpest drop is the percentage of funds devoted to instruction, declining from roughly 50 to 38 percent of the budget. Spending on operation and maintenance of the physical plant also declined, falling from 16 to 12 percent of operating expense. The increases came in general administration (18 to 26 percent) and in student services (9 to 12 percent). The direction of these changes is not particularly surprising to those who know private colleges; administrative demands have grown more complex, and increased responsibilities and growing competition have spurred

4. National Federation of College and University Business Officers Associations, *The Sixty College Study: A Second Look* (Washington, 1960), p. 1.
5. Fiscal 1989 data are taken from the Integrated Postsecondary Education Data Survey (IPEDS), collected by the Department of Education. Data from this source were available for 41 of the 56 colleges included in the 1958 study.

Table 4-1. *Comparison of Revenue and Expenditure,*
Fifty-six Colleges, 1958–89[a]
Percent

	Average		Median	
Item	1958	1989	1958	1989
	Revenue			
Tuition and fees	56.80	54.20	58.60	55.80
Government	n.a.	6.80	n.a.	4.10
Endowment	20.70	18.00	17.60	16.70
Gifts and grants	17.60	13.70	14.20	12.30
Other	2.90	4.20	2.30	3.90
	Expenditure			
Instruction	49.80	37.80	49.60	38.10
Administration	17.60	26.20	19.00	26.00
Operation and maintenance, plant	16.40	11.80	16.60	11.30
Student services	9.20	12.00	9.40	12.00
Libraries	4.80	4.70	4.90	4.30
Research	2.10	2.80	1.10	1.30

Source: The 1958 data are from the National Federation of College and University Business Officers Associations, *The Sixty College Study: A Second Look* (Washington, 1960), pp. 128–33; and the 1989 data, based on 41 colleges, are from the Williams College Project on the Economics of Higher Education. See appendix B.

n.a. Not available.

a. Several adjustments were required to render the 1958 and 1969 data comparable. For expenditures, categories of administrative expense were defined differently in the two years, so several categories are combined into one item, administration, covering public service, academic support, and institutional support. Student aid was not included as an educational and general expenditure in 1958 but was reported separately "below the line," with other expenses such as auxiliary enterprises. For 1989, student aid was subtracted from revenue and expenditure sides of the ledger before computing the percentages in table 4-1. Use of average and median data results in figures that do not add to 100 percent.

Table 4-2. *Student Aid as a Percent of Tuition, Expenditure,*
and Income, Fifty-six Colleges, 1958–89

	Average		Median	
Item	1958	1989	1958	1989
Tuition revenue	7.60	16.40	8.90	14.00
E&G expenditure	10.20	18.80	10.70	16.40
E&G income	4.20	9.40	4.50	8.40

Source: See table 4-1.

growth in administrative functions such as development, admissions, student aid, and student services. Thirty years ago a small administrative team could run a liberal arts college, but that is no longer possible. There are surely those, however, who lament the passing of that era.

Table 4-2 focuses on three indexes of student aid and its growth over three decades. As a percentage of gross tuition revenue in these colleges, average expenditures more than doubled from 7.6 to 16.4 percent. Comparable gains are displayed in the other two measures, student aid as a percentage of E&G expenditure, and of E&G income. Given the dramatic changes that have occurred over these three decades, with student aid increasing to promote equal educational opportunity and to maintain enrollments, one might have expected an even more pronounced shift in expenditure patterns. These data provide another window on the complex issue of determining a financially prudent level of student aid. I would argue that they are consistent with the discussion in chapter 3 that, as of 1989, growth of unfunded student aid had not forced most private colleges into an economically disastrous operating position.

Change during the Past Decade

For the remaining analyses in this chapter a specialized data set assembled by the Williams College Project on the Economics of Higher Education is drawn on.[6] All financial figures are adjusted for inflation and are presented in 1990–91 dollars. Extensive work was done to clean the data sets of reporting and recording errors. The Williams data base covers 181 of the 212 colleges included in this study.

Appendix D gives fuller definitions of the variables included in the tables in this chapter. The variables generally follow standard accounting definitions, but a few were adjusted to reflect an economic rather than an accounting view of financial relationships. As noted earlier, unfunded student aid has been subtracted from revenue and expenditure sides of the budget, putting the focus on net tuition revenue and eliminating student aid from calculations of operating expense. The resulting analyses reflect economic reality more accurately than the standard accounting format.

6. As described in appendix B, the Williams data set, covering fiscal 1979 and 1989, was created by merging data from three national sources: the Higher Education General Information Survey (HEGIS) for 1979, and the Integrated Postsecondary Education Data System (IPEDS) for 1989 (for revenue and expenditure data); the Fiscal-Operations Report and Application to Participate (FISAP) database (for additional data on federal student aid programs); and the HEGIS and IPEDS enrollment surveys (for enrollment data used in calculating full-time-equivalent [FTE] enrollments). Blasdell, McPherson, and Schapiro, "Trends in Revenues and Expenditures," pp. 1–2.

The other variable that has been modified from the conventional accounting form is the revenue labeled gifts and endowment, which has been combined into a single entry. Interest and dividends are only part of the endowment earnings included in this new variable. Besides earnings, the variable includes gifts to endowment and realized and unrealized capital gains. This new variable attempts to capture more accurately the value to the college of its wealth, as reflected in the capital value of the endowment. As a result of this redefinition, the variable gifts and endowment is larger than it would have been were it defined solely as the sum of annual gifts plus interest and dividends.[7] Because each college develops its own policy on the amount to be spent from endowment (the spending rate), this variable does not measure the amount actually spent on education from these sources; colleges typically retain and invest a share of the enhanced value of endowment to increase its value further. In the tables that follow, therefore, gifts and endowment overstates the amount that colleges actually spent from this source. Consequently, one should not assume that net revenue (which includes gifts and endowment) will be approximately equal to net spending. Net revenue will usually be larger.[8] It is most accurate to interpret gifts and endowment as a partial index of the changing wealth of the college, reflecting its ability to spend on current educational services and generate savings that can be used to maintain the real value of the endowment.

All Colleges

Table 4-3 presents revenue and expenditure per FTE student for 181 colleges in fiscal 1979 and 1989. The table also includes the annual real growth of each variable over the decade, as well as the share of each component of net revenue and net expenditure. Net revenue grew substantially, 4.6 percent annually during this decade, driven by a sharp annual increase in the real value of gifts and endowment (up 6.8

7. For a discussion of the economic concepts underlying this change in accounting, see Gordon Winston, "The Necessary Revolution in Financial Accounting," *Planning for Higher Education*, vol. 20 (Summer 1992), pp. 1–16. A complete analysis would also include capital costs, including changing value of the physical plant. The ten-year comparison (1979–89) is sensitive to the values of the stock market, which gained an average of 17 percent a year over the decade.

8. When net revenue (as defined) is less than net spending, then the real value of the endowment is being reduced.

Table 4-3. *Revenue and Expenditure, 181 Colleges, Fiscal 1979–89*
Constant 1990–91 dollars unless noted otherwise

Financial variable[a]	Revenue or expenditure		Annual change (%)	Share of revenue or expenditure (%)	
	1979	1989	1979–89	1979	1989
	Revenue				
Net revenue	10,737	16,835	4.60	100.00	100.00
Net tuition and fees	5,792	7,922	3.20	53.90	47.10
Gifts and endowment	4,259	8,202	6.80	39.70	48.70
Federal grants and contracts	479	366	–2.70	4.50	2.20
State and local grants and contracts	110	276	9.60	1.00	1.60
State and local appropriations	97	69	–3.30	0.90	0.40
Gross tuition and fees	7,021	10,548	4.20	...	...
Total scholarship aid from institutional funds	1,230	2,626	7.90	...	...
Pell and SEOG grants	491	450	–0.90	...	...
	Expenditure				
Net spending	9,635	12,911	3.00	100.00	100.00
Instruction and self-supported research	4,039	5,129	2.40	41.90	39.70
Research	194	229	1.70	2.00	1.80
Public service	89	99	1.10	0.90	0.80
Academic support	340	676	7.10	3.50	5.20
Library	486	521	0.70	5.00	4.00
Student services	1,040	1,635	4.60	10.80	12.70
Institutional support	1,841	2,702	3.90	19.10	20.90
Operation and maintenance	1,389	1,633	1.60	14.40	12.60
Other	217	287	2.80	2.30	2.20
Scholarships, unrestricted	676	1,739	9.90	...	...
Scholarships, restricted	1,045	1,337	2.50	...	...
Plant additions	998	2,336	8.90	...	...

Source: Williams College Project on the Economics of Higher Education.
a. Calculated per full-time equivalent (FTE) student. See appendix D for a more complete definition of each variable.

percent) and net tuition and fees (up 3.2 percent).[9] Total scholarship
support from institutional sources grew at nearly 8 percent annually,
while federal financial aid dropped in real terms by nearly 1 percent
each year.

On the expenditure side, net spending for each student increased
by 3.0 percent a year in real terms, roughly matched by the 3.2 percent
annual growth of net tuition and fees.[10] Three components of expense
grew more rapidly than overall spending—academic support (7.1 percent), student services (4.6 percent), and institutional support (3.9
percent). Spending on libraries (0.7 percent) and on operation and
maintenance of the physical plant (1.6 percent) were among activities
that lost ground in the budget. Unfunded student aid grew rapidly at
9.9 percent a year, while additions to the physical plant were up sharply
(8.9 percent a year).

Overall, these data paint a picture of a financially sound group of
colleges, with key revenue sources growing more rapidly than outlays.
The sharp rise in unfunded student aid, a source of much concern on
campus, did not reduce the growth of net tuition revenue below the
rate of increase of spending, indicating that the pricing strategies
discussed in chapter 3 have been "successful." The danger points in
such aggregate data are the modest growth in spending on libraries (an
issue of educational quality) and on maintenance of physical plant;
deferred maintenance may become a growing problem, given the sharp
increase in spending for new plant.

Ten College Groups

Tables 4-4 and 4-5 present selected revenue and expenditure data for
each FTE student for each of the ten sets of colleges, grouped by
financial and market strength.[11] How did various groups of colleges

9. Remember that this increase in tuition and fees is net of student aid and is in
inflation-adjusted dollars. Putting all values in dollars per FTE student eliminates evidence
on economies of scale.

10. These data confirm, over a longer period of years, the analyses in chapter 3,
which showed that growth in educational spending was matched (or exceeded) by growth
in net tuition revenue.

11. See appendix B for details. The Williams data set includes 181 of the 190 colleges
that I was able to rank. The nine ranked colleges not part of the Williams data are Carroll,
Hampshire, Agnes Scott, Wabash, Kalamazoo, Houghton, Roanoke, Presbyterian, and
King colleges.

Table 4-4. *Selected Revenue Items, Ten College Groups, 1979–89*[a]

Constant 1990–91 dollars unless noted otherwise

Item	Group									
	One	Two	Three	Four	Five	Six	Seven	Eight	Nine	Ten
Net revenue										
1979	14,343	12,992	12,842	9,531	10,877	9,522	8,719	8,408	9,792	7,245
1989	30,627	22,523	18,719	12,403	15,567	11,175	11,628	11,195	10,255	7,579
Percent change	7.90	5.70	3.80	2.70	3.70	1.60	2.90	2.90	0.50	0.50
Net tuition and fees										
1979	7,495	6,903	6,549	5,873	5,466	4,681	3,900	4,466	4,647	3,385
1989	11,072	9,664	9,427	7,705	7,066	6,259	5,288	5,557	5,164	4,141
Percent change	4.00	3.40	3.70	2.80	2.60	2.90	3.10	2.20	1.10	2.00
Gifts and endowments										
1979	6,042	5,575	5,534	3,080	4,886	4,369	3,744	3,164	4,364	2,986
1989	18,837	12,303	8,677	4,065	7,682	4,241	5,292	4,790	4,133	2,538
Percent change	12.00	8.20	4.60	2.80	4.60	−0.30	3.50	4.20	−0.50	−1.60
Gross tuition and fees										
1979	9,088	8,195	7,957	7,128	6,798	5,853	5,540	5,383	5,535	4,363
1989	14,397	12,917	12,113	10,674	10,338	8,416	7,410	7,639	7,279	5,918
Percent change	4.70	4.70	4.30	4.10	4.30	3.70	3.00	3.60	2.80	3.10
Total scholarship aid from institutional funds										
1979	1,593	1,292	1,408	1,254	1,332	1,172	1,640	917	888	978
1989	3,325	3,252	2,687	2,969	3,272	2,157	2,122	2,082	2,114	1,777
Percent change	7.60	9.70	6.70	9.00	9.40	6.30	2.60	8.50	9.10	6.20
Pell and SEOG grants										
1979	337	322	303	411	478	586	1,132	557	712	1,050
1989	314	315	319	406	489	487	839	596	682	856
Percent change	−0.70	−0.20	0.50	−0.10	0.20	−1.80	−3.00	0.70	−0.40	−2.00

Source: See table 4-3. Percent changes are annual averages.

a. Calculated per FTE student.

Table 4-5. *Selected Expenditure Items, Ten College Groups, 1979–89*[a]
Constant 1990–91 dollars unless noted otherwise

Item	Group									
	One	Two	Three	Four	Five	Six	Seven	Eight	Nine	Ten
Net spending										
1979	13,326	10,637	10,314	9,956	9,415	8,155	9,452	8,120	8,621	7,206
1989	19,795	15,871	14,170	12,972	12,125	10,182	9,696	10,455	9,586	7,933
Percent change	4.00	4.10	3.20	2.70	2.60	2.20	0.30	2.60	1.10	1.00
Instruction, self-supported research										
1979	5,499	4,558	4,357	4,045	3,885	3,149	3,979	3,079	3,272	2,767
1989	7,690	6,414	5,823	5,059	4,798	3,564	3,619	3,628	3,571	2,939
Percent change	3.40	3.50	2.90	2.30	2.10	1.20	-0.90	1.70	0.90	0.60
Academic support										
1979	639	366	248	239	265	419	319	236	432	226
1989	1,301	924	586	699	600	561	351	418	436	277
Percent change	7.40	9.70	9.00	11.30	8.50	3.00	1.00	5.90	0.10	2.10
Library										
1979	875	586	443	430	432	341	384	416	331	327
1989	928	694	649	411	415	403	322	321	289	277
Percent change	0.60	1.70	3.90	-0.50	-0.40	1.70	-1.70	-2.60	-1.30	-1.60
Student services										
1979	1,401	1,170	1,127	1,055	1,123	978	855	1,056	1,134	916
1989	2,357	1,922	1,972	1,697	1,749	1,457	1,180	1,567	1,493	1,149
Percent change	5.30	5.10	5.80	4.90	4.50	4.10	3.30	4.00	2.80	2.30

Institutional support										
1979	2,256	1,874	2,243	2,200	1,929	1,595	1,911	1,848	1,735	1,676
1989	3,792	3,242	3,049	3,012	2,484	2,304	2,251	2,680	2,075	2,059
Percent change	5.30	5.60	3.10	3.20	2.60	3.70	1.70	3.80	1.80	2.10
Operation and maintenance										
1979	1,879	1,519	1,382	1,575	1,481	1,395	1,387	1,102	1,278	1,018
1989	2,415	1,810	1,795	1,664	1,529	1,553	1,578	1,347	1,226	1,044
Percent change	2.50	1.80	2.60	0.60	0.30	1.10	1.30	2.00	-0.40	0.30
Scholarships, unrestricted										
1979	723	702	725	729	781	638	704	538	615	579
1989	1,875	2,208	1,699	2,063	2,317	1,325	1,387	1,342	1,314	1,324
Percent change	10.00	12.10	8.90	11.00	11.50	7.60	7.00	9.60	7.90	8.60
Scholarships, restricted										
1979	1,207	912	986	937	1,029	1,119	2,068	936	985	1,448
1989	1,763	1,360	1,306	1,311	1,443	1,319	1,574	1,335	1,483	1,309
Percent change	3.90	4.10	2.90	3.40	3.40	1.70	-2.70	3.60	4.20	-1.00
Plant additions										
1979	1,784	979	1,352	563	934	1,150	432	364	623	468
1989	3,591	2,883	2,909	2,432	1,723	1,456	1,994	1,185	1,022	973
Percent change	7.20	11.40	8.00	15.80	6.30	2.40	16.50	12.50	5.10	7.60

Source: See table 4-3.
a. Calculated per FTE student. Percent changes are annual averages.

fare in the 1980s? Did the strongest colleges gain in relative strength, did the weakest colleges slip further back or hold their own, and what was the experience of those in the middle tiers?

Clearly, the stronger colleges enhanced their relative standing, largely through exceptional growth in gifts and endowment. Group 1 colleges posted a 12 percent annual gain in that category, and group 2 an 8.2 percent gain, while groups 6, 9, and 10 lost value in real terms, with negative growth rates. The stronger colleges also had larger gains in net tuition and fees, although the spread here is less pronounced— 4.0 percent annual gain for group 1 versus a low of 1.1 percent for group 9. The overall result was an average growth of net revenue per student of nearly 8 percent annually in group 1 and 5.7 percent in group 2, while groups 9 and 10 increased at only 0.5 percent. In 1979, the ratio of net revenue per student between group 1 and group 10 was roughly two to one; by 1989, that ratio had doubled to four to one ($30,627 versus $7,579).

The differences in annual growth rates of gross tuition and fees were smaller, however, ranging from 4.7 percent in groups 1 and 2, to a low of 2.8 percent in group 9. Similarly, the growth of financial aid from institutional sources varied little across the groups, with an average gain of nearly 8 percent a year; the one exception to this pattern was group 7, where the annual increase was only 2.6 percent. The drop in federal financial aid was experienced more or less equally by all groups as well.

Table 4-5 shows a similar pattern for expenditures; net spending per FTE student grew more rapidly in the stronger colleges, with increases of 4 percent annually in groups 1 and 2, compared with 1 percent in groups 9 and 10. In 1979, group 1 colleges spent approximately 1.8 times as much for each student as group 10 colleges; by 1989, they were spending 2.5 times as much ($19,795 versus $7,933). Library spending generally grew little, if at all, in any of the groups, except for group 3, where annual growth was nearly 4 percent. Spending on student services increased in every group, with rates ranging from 5.8 percent in group 3 to 2.3 percent in group 10 colleges. Increased outlays on institutional support ranged from a high of 5.6 percent in group 2 to a low of 1.7 percent in group 7, with groups 9 and 10 also near the low end at roughly 2 percent. The highest growth rate of spending for operation and maintenance of physical plant was 2.6 percent in group

3, with groups 4, 5, 9, and 10 below 1 percent. All groups of colleges appear to have sought budgetary savings through deferred maintenance.

Scholarships from unrestricted funds (unfunded student aid) grew sharply at all colleges, and at much faster rates than did grants from restricted funds. While securing new endowments to support financial aid is a high priority for most colleges, no group seems to have made much headway during the 1980s. Additions to plant and equipment, however, showed sharp increases in several of the groups, particularly group 2 (11.4 percent), 4 (15.8 percent), 7 (16.5 percent), and 8 (12.5 percent). Only group 6, with an annual increase of 2.4 percent, seems to have resisted the temptation to expand plant capacity significantly.

A comparison of net revenue with net expenditure for 1989 reveals several interesting patterns. Groups 1, 2, and 3 have much higher net revenue per student than net expense, reflecting primarily the wealth of these colleges. In group 4 colleges, however, net revenue per student is less than net spending ($12,403 versus $12,972), attributable on the revenue side to relatively low net tuition and fees, as well as sharply lower gift and endowment income. These data highlight the dilemma of colleges in the middle tier; they seek to enroll very good students and thus must be competitive with their academic and extracurricular programs, but they do not have the financial resources of the wealthier colleges.[12] Middle-tier colleges, therefore, are forced to spend more than their resources prudently permit to attract a share of the highest quality students.[13] The only other case where net revenue per student is less than net spending is group 10 ($7,579 versus $7,933), where limited income from tuition and gifts and endowment simply leaves these colleges in very difficult financial straits. Finally, in groups 6, 9, and 10, the annual growth of net revenues was less than the growth in net spending. If that pattern continues, the financial situation of these colleges will continue to deteriorate.

Women's Colleges

Revenue and expenditure data for 23 women's colleges are presented in table 4-6. As a group, these colleges seem stronger financially in

12. This issue was also noted in connection with analyses in chapter 3.
13. Alternatively, these colleges could redefine the market niche in which they are competing.

Table 4-6. *Revenue and Expenditure, Twenty-three Women's Colleges, Fiscal 1979–89*[a]
Constant 1990–91 dollars unless noted otherwise

Financial variable	Revenue or expenditure		Annual change (%)	Share of revenue or expenditure (%)	
	1979	1989	1979–89	1979	1989
Revenue					
Net revenue	11,312	18,474	5.00	100.00	100.00
Net tuition and fees	5,601	7,058	2.30	49.50	38.20
Gifts and endowment	4,957	10,638	7.90	43.80	57.60
Federal grants and contracts	572	427	−2.90	5.10	2.30
State and local grants and contracts	147	299	7.40	1.30	1.60
State and local appropriations	35	52	4.00	0.30	0.30
Gross tuition and fees	6,860	9,626	3.40	...	...
Total scholarship aid from institutional funds	1,259	2,565	7.40	...	...
Pell and SEOG grants	517	383	−3.00	...	...
Expenditure					
Net spending	11,080	14,256	2.60	100.00	100.00
Instruction and self-supported research	4,169	5,309	2.40	37.60	37.20
Research	247	318	2.60	2.20	2.20
Public service	160	125	−2.40	1.40	0.90
Academic support	553	940	5.40	5.00	6.60
Library	527	442	−1.70	4.80	3.10
Student services	1,200	1,835	4.30	10.80	12.90
Institutional support	2,220	3,111	3.40	20.00	21.80
Operation and maintenance	1,779	1,884	0.60	16.10	13.20
Other	225	292	2.60	2.00	2.00
Scholarships from unrestricted funds	520	1,420	10.60	...	...
Scholarships from restricted funds	1,256	1,527	2.00	...	...
Plant additions	734	1,873	9.80	...	...

Source: See table 4-3.
a. Calculated per FTE student.

1989 than a decade earlier, for net revenue per student in 1989 ($18,474) exceeds net expense ($14,256) substantially, while in 1979, the two figures were virtually equal. (Net revenue in these colleges grew 5.0 percent annually over the decade, while net spending increased by only 2.6 percent.) The explanation is to be found in the substantial growth of gifts and endowment (7.9 percent), which exceeds the 6.8 percent gain recorded by all colleges in this study. Net tuition and fees did not fare as well, increasing by only 2.3 percent annually, but growth in net spending (2.6 percent) was held below that of all colleges (3.0 percent). Outlays on libraries (− 1.7 percent) and operation and maintenance of plant (0.6 percent) were below the overall rates, suggesting that short-term budgetary savings were realized in these areas.

Women's colleges have received considerable attention in recent years, with the furor over coeducation at Mills College in California the most obvious example. More will be said about prospects for women's colleges in chapter 6, but these 23 colleges did gain in financial strength during the 1980s.

Black Colleges

Nine historically black colleges are represented in the Williams data base, with revenue and expenditure data reported in table 4-7. For these colleges, a very different story is revealed. Net revenue barely increased in real terms, growing by only 0.7 percent annually, while net spending declined in constant dollars from $10,412 in 1979 to $9,149 in 1989, a drop of 1.3 percent annually. Spending on instruction, academic support, student services, and the library declined in real terms. Financial aid from institutional sources fell sharply (− 4.8 percent a year), as did federal financial aid (− 4.2 percent a year). On the revenue side, net tuition and fees grew 2.5 percent yearly but remained at the extremely low level in 1989 of $3,625. Gifts and endowments were also at a low level ($4,014 in 1989), having grown at only 1.1 percent a year. Federal grants and contracts are of great importance to these colleges, amounting to $2,425 for each student in 1979, and $2,013 in 1989. The program that supplies most of these federal dollars is Title III of the Higher Education Act, Aid to Developing Institutions. Without these dollars many private black colleges could not survive. That federal support dropped by nearly 2 percent annually in real terms was surely felt on these campuses. The only visible financial

Table 4-7. *Revenue and Expenditure, Nine Black Colleges, 1979–89*[a]
Constant 1990–91 dollars unless noted otherwise

Financial variable	Revenue or expenditure		Annual change (%)	Share of revenue or expenditure (%)	
	1979	1989	1979–89	1979	1989
			Revenue		
Net revenue	9,286	9,979	0.70	100.00	100.00
Net tuition and fees	2,844	3,625	2.50	30.60	36.30
Gifts and endowment	3,605	4,014	1.10	38.80	40.20
Federal grants and contracts	2,425	2,013	–1.80	26.10	20.20
State and local grants and contracts	325	213	–4.10	3.50	2.10
State and local appropriations	87	114	2.70	0.90	1.10
Gross tuition and fees	4,466	4,616	0.30	...	...
Total scholarship aid, institutional funds	1,621	991	–4.80	...	...
Pell and SEOG grants	2,673	1,736	–4.20	...	...
			Expenditure		
Net spending	10,412	9,149	–1.30	100.00	100.00
Instruction and self-supported research	4,030	2,956	–3.10	38.70	32.30
Research	228	408	6.00	2.20	4.50
Public service	307	93	–11.30	2.90	1.00
Academic support	566	377	–4.00	5.40	4.10
Library	315	252	–2.20	3.00	2.80
Student services	1,174	904	–2.60	11.30	9.90
Institutional support	2,301	2,410	0.50	22.10	26.30
Operation and maintenance	1,271	1,674	2.80	12.20	18.30
Other	220	75	–10.20	2.10	0.80
Scholarships, unrestricted funds	556	530	–0.50	...	...
Scholarships, restricted funds	3,738	2,196	–5.20	...	...
Plant additions	487	1,122	8.70	...	...

Source: See table 4-3.
a. Calculated per FTE student.

improvement is that budget cuts have brought net spending down far enough to be covered by net revenue, but at what cost to quality? These colleges have a history of surviving, however, and one should not count them out.[14]

Religiously Affiliated Colleges

Tables 4-8, 4-9, and 4-10 examine financial data from colleges affiliated with the Roman Catholic, Presbyterian, and Methodist churches. The picture portrayed for 17 Catholic colleges is one of financial balance (though worsening slightly over the decade) and relative austerity (table 4-8). Net revenue between 1979 and 1989 grew by only 1.8 percent annually, while net spending increased by 2.5 percent, a pattern that is troubling. Compared with many liberal arts colleges, the level of gifts and endowment is low and grew by only 0.7 percent a year during a decade when the average rate for colleges in this study was nearly 7 percent. Net tuition and fees is also low relative to all colleges ($6,504 versus $7,922 in 1989). Unfunded student aid, however, increased at below-average rates, suggesting that Catholic colleges chose not to discount as much as peer institutions or were not forced to do so. Overall, the data depict a group of Catholic colleges that are not wealthy but that operate frugally and generally live within their means.

Table 4-9 presents data on 22 Presbyterian colleges. Net revenue for these schools grew 2.3 percent a year, exceeding net spending (1.7 percent), yielding a modest improvement in financial condition. Levels of net tuition and fees and gifts and endowment are lower than the average for all colleges in the study, as were the growth rates for these two income variables. Increased spending was equally modest, however, preserving financial balance. Unfunded student aid did grow at the fairly high rate of 11.6 percent, indicating that these colleges have discounted tuition sharply to maintain enrollments or to attract particular students to their campuses.

Table 4-10 provides financial information on 25 Methodist colleges. As with the Presbyterian schools, the general picture is one of financial balance and austerity. Net revenue and net spending increased by roughly similar amounts, 2.1 and 2.3 percent, respectively. Both major

14. One apparent success story is Fisk University. See chapters 5 and 6 in this volume.

Table 4-8. *Revenue and Expenditure, Seventeen Catholic Colleges, 1979–89*[a]
Constant 1990–91 dollars unless noted otherwise

Financial variable	Revenue or expenditure		Annual change (%)	Share of revenue or expenditure (%)	
	1979	1989	1979–89	1979	1989
Revenue					
Net revenue	9,947	11,870	1.80	100.00	100.00
Net tuition and fees	4,557	6,504	3.60	45.80	54.80
Gifts and endowment	4,155	4,438	0.70	41.80	37.40
Federal grants and contracts	934	417	–7.70	9.40	3.50
State and local grants and contracts	252	447	5.90	2.50	3.80
State and local appropriations	49	64	2.70	0.50	0.50
Gross tuition and fees	5,509	8,099	3.90	. . .	. . .
Total scholarship aid, institutional funds	952	1,595	5.30	. . .	. . .
Pell and SEOG grants[b]	547	440	–2.20	. . .	. . .
Expenditure					
Net spending	8,058	10,327	2.50	100.00	100.00
Instruction and self-supported research	3,107	3,548	1.30	38.60	34.40
Research	176	141	–2.20	2.20	1.40
Public service	67	51	–2.70	0.80	0.50
Academic support	496	534	0.70	6.20	5.20
Library	364	346	–0.50	4.50	3.40
Student services	930	1,379	4.00	11.50	13.40
Institutional support	1,633	2,592	4.70	20.30	25.10
Operation and maintenance	1,186	1,384	1.60	14.70	13.40
Other	99	352	13.50	1.20	3.40
Scholarships, unrestricted funds	567	1,045	6.30	. . .	. . .
Scholarships, restricted funds	933	990	0.60	. . .	. . .
Plant additions	519	1,641	12.20	. . .	. . .

Source: See table 4-3.
a. Calculated per FTE student.

Table 4-9. *Revenue and Expenditure, Twenty-two Presbyterian Colleges, 1979–89*[a]
Constant 1990–91 dollars unless noted otherwise

Financial variable	Revenue or expenditure		Annual change (%) 1979–89	Share of revenue or expenditure (%)	
	1979	1989		1979	1989
Revenue					
Net revenue	10,433	13,134	2.30	100.00	100.00
Net tuition and fees	4,926	6,161	2.30	47.20	46.90
Gifts and endowment	4,804	6,345	2.80	46.00	48.30
Federal grants and contracts	497	273	−5.80	4.80	2.10
State and local grants and contracts	183	332	6.10	1.80	2.50
State and local appropriations	23	23	0.00	0.20	0.20
Gross tuition and fees	6,282	9,029	3.70	...	...
Total scholarship aid, institutional funds	1,356	2,868	7.80	...	...
Pell and SEOG grants[b]	671	575	−1.50	...	...
Expenditure					
Net spending	9,647	11,440	1.70	100.00	100.00
Instruction and self-supported research	3,995	4,499	1.20	41.40	39.30
Research	31	40	2.60	0.30	0.30
Public service	41	43	0.50	0.40	0.40
Academic support	306	502	5.10	3.20	4.40
Library	455	404	−1.20	4.70	3.50
Student services	1,116	1,761	4.70	11.60	15.40
Institutional support	2,036	2,388	1.60	21.10	20.90
Operation and maintenance	1,465	1,569	0.70	15.20	13.70
Other	202	234	1.50	2.10	2.00
Scholarships, unrestricted funds	655	1,967	11.60	...	...
Scholarships, restricted funds	1,373	1,476	0.70	...	...
Plant additions	867	2,066	9.10	...	...

Source: See table 4-3.
a. Calculated per FTE student.

Table 4-10. *Revenue and Expenditure, Twenty-five Methodist Colleges, 1979–89*[a]

Constant 1990–91 dollars unless noted otherwise

Financial variable	Revenue or expenditure		Annual change (%) 1979–89	Share of revenue or expenditure (%)	
	1979	1989		1979	1989
Revenue					
Net revenue	9,618	11,892	2.10	100.00	100.00
Net tuition and fees	4,375	5,673	2.60	45.50	47.70
Gifts and endowment	4,770	5,469	1.40	49.60	46.00
Federal grants and contracts	327	266	-2.00	3.40	2.20
State and local grants and contracts	99	471	16.90	1.00	4.00
State and local appropriations	47	13	-12.10	0.50	0.10
Gross tuition and fees	5,514	8,062	3.90	...	...
Total scholarship aid, institutional funds	1,139	2,389	7.70	...	...
Pell and SEOG grants	524	514	-0.20	...	...
Expenditure					
Net spending	7,884	9,902	2.30	100.00	100.00
Instruction and self-supported research	3,299	3,920	1.70	41.80	39.60
Research	53	26	-6.90	0.70	0.30
Public service	57	88	4.40	0.70	0.90
Academic support	166	422	9.80	2.10	4.30
Library	402	416	0.30	5.10	4.20
Student services	887	1,328	4.10	11.30	13.40
Institutional support	1,529	2,118	3.30	19.40	21.40
Operation and maintenance	1,339	1,415	0.60	17.00	14.30
Other	152	169	1.10	1.90	1.70
Scholarships, unrestricted funds	620	1,501	9.20	...	...
Scholarships, restricted funds	1,043	1,402	3.00	...	...
Plant additions	673	2,017	11.60	...	...

Source: See table 4-3.

a. Calculated per FTE student.

sources of income—net tuition and fees, and gifts and endowment—
were at low levels compared with all colleges, and experienced below-
average growth rates; spending increases, however, were also kept in
check. In fact, net spending for each student in 1989 ($9,904) was a
full $3,000 lower than the $12,911 average for all colleges in this study.
Unfunded student aid in Methodist colleges grew at roughly the average
rate for all colleges in the study.

The overriding impression from data on these religiously affiliated
colleges is that they are surviving financially but with income and
wealth substantially below average for the sector. Financial support
from the denominations is not large, and the religious tie may hinder
fund-raising if ministers or other denominational representatives take
up several positions on the board of trustees. Whatever the explanation,
these data clearly show that the financially stronger colleges are generally those that no longer have an explicit tie with a religious denomination.

Conclusion

These data reveal the extremes of wealth and expenditure per
student that exist in the universe of liberal arts colleges. The 1980s
were especially beneficial to those colleges with sizable endowments,
for the growth of financial assets was extraordinary. As a result,
however, the gulf separating the wealthiest and poorest colleges grew
substantially, not unlike the pattern among individuals.

Among the ten groups of colleges, the bottom two (groups 9 and
10) have troubling financial profiles, with net revenue increasing by
only 0.5 percent a year, while spending rose by 1 percent annually. At
a different level, colleges in group 4 collectively spent more per student
than they received in net revenue, presumably leading to some erosion
in endowment values. Women's colleges as a group experienced re-
markably good financial results, ending the decade much stronger than
they entered it. The nine historically black colleges in the data set
exhibit bleak financial profiles and have obviously had to slash spending
to survive. The three groups of religiously affiliated colleges seem to
be in financial balance but at the low end of the wealth scale. As these
variations make clear, liberal arts colleges do not face a common
future.

CHAPTER FIVE

Site Visits

To GAIN insight into how administrators at liberal arts colleges see the prospects and problems facing their institutions, I visited 12 colleges in the winter and spring of 1992. The colleges—Bowdoin, Bradford, Colorado College, Dickinson, Fisk, Guilford, Hollins, Knox, Olivet, Union, Westmont, and Wittenberg—include eight Liberal Arts I and four Liberal Arts II institutions as classified by the Carnegie Foundation. Twelve states are represented—Maine, Massachusetts, Colorado, Pennsylvania, Tennessee, North Carolina, Virginia, Illinois, Michigan, New York, California, and Ohio—and the group includes one women's college (Hollins), one historically black college (Fisk), and one evangelical Christian college (Westmont). I tried to select a broadly representative group, believing that the issues identified would be found on most campuses in this sector; visits to additional colleges, however, would no doubt add nuance as well as unique situations.

My focus in these one-day visits was on the future, not the past. I wanted to learn what campus officials were thinking about, what worried them most, and how they were planning to meet the challenges they foresee in future years. Inevitably, our discussions touched on the past, but my purpose was not to gather data or interpret the unique stories of each college. Instead, I sought common themes, issues that cut across several campuses, as well as approaches to problem solving and management that were new and promising. As a result, my findings are organized around broad themes, with examples drawn from particular colleges visited.

The Twelve Colleges

Table 5-1 provides information on the three measures I used to assess financial and enrollment strength for all 212 colleges included

Table 5-1. *Rankings of Twelve Colleges by Net Tuition, Endowment, and Acceptances*

Group	Institution	Net tuition[a] ($)	Rank	Endowment[a]	Rank	Percent of applicants accepted	Rank	Overall rank
1	Bowdoin College	11,661	8	101,661	12	22	3	3
2	Colorado College	9,385	43	62,446	32	35	15	21
2	Union College	10,075	35	38,736	50	39	21	25
2	Dickinson College	10,376	28	22,010	85	40	22	32
3	Hollins College	8,118	65	40,903	46	73	95	55
5	Wittenberg University	7,854	69	17,039	104	71	91	78
5	Knox College	7,337	79	25,990	76	77	112	80
5	Bradford College	6,719	96	16,907	105	74	100	91
5	Guilford College	6,340	114	13,735	115	65	75	94
8	Westmont College	6,716	97	5,130	165	78	115	137
8	Fisk University	4,251	169	4,890	166	63	67	152
10	Olivet College	4,790	155	7,832	145	94	186	180

Sources: Author's calculations based on data from the College Board, New York, and the National Center for Higher Education Systems, Boulder, Colorado. See appendix A.
a. Calculated per full-time-equivalent (FTE) student.

Table 5-2. *Tuition in Twelve Colleges, Selected Years, 1978–91*

Group	Institution	1978	1983	1988	1989	1990	1991
1	Bowdoin College	4,180	7,665	11,515	12,565	14,060	15,320
2	Dickinson College	3,780	6,715	11,340	12,230	13,400	14,600
2	Union College	4,275	7,399	11,103	12,313	13,513	14,578
2	Colorado College	3,600	6,400	9,505	10,240	11,470	12,710
5	Wittenberg University	3,185	6,266	9,855	10,702	11,754	12,072
5	Knox College	3,950	6,435	9,120	9,822	10,746	11,559
8	Westmont College	2,900	5,490	8,030	8,670	9,780	10,900
3	Hollins College	3,850	5,450	8,736	9,357	9,900	10,810
5	Bradford College	3,400	5,800	8,600	9,100	10,010	10,810
5	Guilford College	2,500	4,350	7,063	7,910	8,690	9,540
10	Olivet College	n.a.	5,120	5,560	6,060	6,860	7,360
8	Fisk University	2,200	4,900	4,315	4,600	4,600	4,950

Source: See table 5-1.

in this study: net tuition for each full-time-equivalent (FTE) student; endowment for each FTE student; and ratio of acceptances to applications. These 12 colleges include one from group 1, three from group 2, one from group 3, four from group 5, two from group 8, and one from group 10. I deliberately oversampled from the middle groups because, as noted in chapter 3, the competitive situation of such colleges is particularly interesting and complex. They compete for very good students but lack the wealth and national prestige of the top colleges. I wanted my interview findings to include a strong representation from colleges positioned in this part of the sector.

Table 5-2 presents the tuitions charged by the 12 colleges for selected years between 1978 and 1991. The wide range in tuitions charged in 1991, from a high of $15,320 at Bowdoin to a low of $4,950 at Fisk, with other rates distributed between, is typical of the sector, and demonstrates how diverse the financial circumstances are among these seemingly similar colleges. Table 5-3 shows net tuition revenue per FTE student for selected years between 1978 and 1989, and the values of beta (unfunded student aid divided by gross tuition revenue per FTE student) for each of those years.[1] The substantial diversity across colleges in net tuition revenue and in the size of unfunded aid is apparent in these figures.

Finally, table 5-4 provides data on applications, acceptances, and entering enrollments for each college for selected years between 1977 and 1991. Selectivity rates (acceptances divided by applications) and yield rates (enrollments divided by acceptances) are also reported. The extremes in market strength found among these 12 colleges reflect the reality within the sector.

Site-Visit Findings

I invited each of the 12 colleges to participate in the study by letter to the president, explaining the nature of my project and stressing my interest in learning about the issues that confront the colleges as they plan for the future. In follow-up telephone calls, I requested copies of any planning documents that had been prepared, as well as other

1. See chapter 3 for full discussion of this measure. Tables 6-1 and 6-2 in chapter 6 provide data on revenue and expenditure in each of the 12 site-visit colleges for 1979 and 1989.

Table 5-3. *Net Tuition Revenue and β, Twelve Colleges, Selected Years, 1978–89*[a]

| Institution | 1978 | | 1983 | | 1988 | | 1989 | |
	Net tuition revenue	β	Net tuition revenue	β	Net tuition revenue	β	Net tuition revenue	β
Bowdoin College	4,000	6	7,008	9	11,402	2	11,661	7
Colorado College	3,555	5	5,958	11	8,775	11	9,386	11
Dickinson College	3,488	10	6,153	10	9,613	14	10,376	15
Hollins College	3,701	10	5,955	12	7,761	12	8,118	11
Knox College	3,808	1	5,723	12	6,677	24	7,337	23
Union College	3,682	9	6,272	9	9,342	11	10,075	13
Bradford College	2,551	17	4,847	19	6,693	12	6,719	19
Guilford College	2,391	7	3,833	8	5,727	10	6,340	11
Westmont College	2,807	11	4,454	18	6,791	16	6,716	17
Wittenberg University	2,997	11	5,270	15	7,084	26	7,854	25
Fisk University	2,030	16	4,462	25	n.a.	12	4,251	7
Olivet College	2,202	16	4,728	7	4,458	17	4,790	17

Source: See table 5-1.
n.a. Not available.
a. Calculated per FTE student; beta expressed in percent.

Table 5-4. *Applications, Acceptances, Enrollments, Selectivity, and Yield, Twelve Colleges, Selected Years, 1977–91*[a]

Item	1977	1983	1989	1991
Bowdoin College				
Applications	3,513	3,122	3,665	3,242
Acceptances	732	820	805	867
Enrollments	375	417	397	406
Selectivity	21	26	22	27
Yield	51	51	49	47
Bradford College				
Applications	487	568	715	533
Acceptances	359	428	530	362
Enrollments	132	99	119	98
Selectivity	74	75	74	68
Yield	37	23	22	27
Colorado College				
Applications	2,174	2,082	3,426	2,770
Acceptances	1,060	1,439	1,200	1,375
Enrollments	554	612	466	494
Selectivity	49	69	35	50
Yield	52	43	39	36
Dickinson College				
Applications	2,018	3,079	4,438	3,639
Acceptances	1,538	1,549	1,766	2,399
Enrollments	502	521	536	556
Selectivity	76	50	40	66
Yield	33	34	30	23
Fisk University				
Applications	944	808	1,052	n.a.
Acceptances	789	618	660	n.a.
Enrollments	325	220	268	n.a.
Selectivity	84	76	63	n.a.
Yield	41	36	41	n.a.
Guilford College				
Applications	1,053	914	1,304	1,180
Acceptances	770	696	846	949
Enrollments	324	306	340	333
Selectivity	73	76	65	80
Yield	42	44	40	35
Hollins College				
Applications	795	850	857	685
Acceptances	627	600	622	559
Enrollments	300	245	231	226
Selectivity	79	71	73	82
Yield	48	41	37	40

Table 5-4 (*continued*)

Item	1977	1983	1989	1991
Knox College				
Applications	732	856	914	796
Acceptances	564	642	707	617
Enrollments	263	255	274	221
Selectivity	77	75	77	78
Yield	47	40	39	36
Olivet College				
Applications	n.a.	489	631	613
Acceptances	n.a.	432	593	610
Enrollments	n.a.	195	359	161
Selectivity	n.a.	88	94	1.00
Yield	n.a.	45	61	26
Union College				
Applications	2,732	3,056	3,437	2,752
Acceptances	1,490	1,317	1,356	1,428
Enrollments	520	533	529	443
Selectivity	55	43	39	52
Yield	35	40	39	31
Westmont College				
Applications	401	391	949	809
Acceptances	320	352	742	648
Enrollments	250	238	391	299
Selectivity	80	90	78	80
Yield	78	68	53	46
Wittenberg University				
Applications	1,831	1,772	2,705	2,418
Acceptances	1,630	1,506	1,924	1,850
Enrollments	684	604	676	622
Selectivity	89	85	71	77
Yield	42	40	35	34

Source: See table 5-1.

a. Selectivity expresses the percent of applicants accepted, and yield expresses the percent of students accepted who enroll.

materials that would help me understand the unique circumstances of each college. I asked to spend one day on campus, interviewing five individuals: the president; the academic vice president, provost, or dean; the director of admissions; the vice president for development; and the chief financial or business officer. I spent approximately one hour in discussion with each of these individuals and occasionally met with another official or faculty member recommended by the president. I received complete cooperation on every campus and in most cases received a wealth of material in advance that made my time on campus highly efficient. No college turned down my request to participate in the study, and I appreciate very much the cooperation and helpful spirit with which my requests were handled. Appendix E in this volume contains the names and positions of the individuals interviewed.

I took notes during the interviews but did not tape record the sessions. Nor did I follow a rigid interview protocol with officials; instead, we simply engaged in an hour's free discussion of issues that were on the minds of the individuals interviewed. In most cases, copies of my letter had been distributed in advance, so it was understood why I was there and what I was seeking. Needless to say, the people with whom I spoke are sophisticated professionals, who spend much of their time working with, and thinking about, the types of concerns in which I was interested, so little time was wasted getting down to substance. That I had served as president of a similar institution also helped the flow of conversation and the ease with which we discussed difficult issues.

After all site visits were completed, I went through my notes and wrote one-line descriptions of each issue that had been raised by the more than sixty individuals with whom I had met. Patterns quickly emerged, and it became apparent that eight categories captured the essence of what was discussed. Those eight categories are (in descending order of number of distinct issues raised) enrollments and students; management and finance; faculty; academic programs; development; planning; trustees; and government policies.

Enrollment and Students

It is hardly surprising that issues surrounding students and enrollments would dominate the conversations, for these colleges are essentially single-purpose institutions, dedicated to the education of undergraduate students. Unlike some of the other topics, virtually all administrators regardless of position had comments about students; their numbers, quality, and financing dominate the institutional agenda.

Concerns about meeting desired enrollment goals were apparent in 8 of the 12 colleges, those from groups 3 and below in the rankings of table 5-1. The four highest-ranked colleges in that table accept less than half of their applicants, while the other eight accept two-thirds or more of their applicants. Although the marketing situation facing each campus in the nation is unique in some respects, a rough rule of thumb might be that whenever a college accepts more than half of its applicants, it has to worry to some degree about meeting its numerical enrollment targets. On that basis, data from table A-2 suggest that concerns about numerical enrollment may be an issue for all but about forty of these colleges. This concern is not just hypothetical; more than half the colleges I visited had recently enrolled fewer students than desired.

Regardless of the college's market position, however, administrators expressed universal concern about increased price resistance from potential students and their families. The weakened economy was singled out as the main cause, coupled with growing uncertainty about job security felt by families that had not faced such worries in the past. Several of those interviewed mentioned the economy as the reason for raising tuition by smaller rates in recent years. Boards of trustees have also been insisting on smaller tuition increases at several of these colleges, reflecting the growing (but age-old) concern about pricing the institution out of its market, as well as the bad public relations created by the sharp increases in the 1980s. The one commonly mentioned offsetting factor was the educational confusion created in many public universities by recent cuts in state appropriations. Widespread reports of students being unable to complete degrees in four years, of major fields being discontinued, and so forth have caused private colleges to look more stable in the eyes of many families, even though tuition is much higher. In California, for example, where both the University of California and California State University systems have experienced sharp budget cuts and enrollment caps, applications in 1992 were up at every private college in the state.

I was surprised that officials on several of the campuses remarked that their college had been slow to adjust to the changing demographics and the declining number of high school graduates in the 1980s and thus had been forced to scramble to make up for lost time. One would have thought that the much-heralded enrollment decline could hardly have been missed, and that few colleges would have failed to move promptly to enhance their recruiting activities, but apparently inertia is a powerful force even on campuses that are heavily dependent on tuition. Most of the campuses were still struggling to increase the enrollment of minority students, but few were reaching the goals they had set.[2] Several of the colleges had begun or expanded programs for

2. Table A-1 shows that most liberal arts colleges have only a small number of black students enrolled.

nontraditional students, that is, part-time, older students, often studying for degrees in separate evening courses or enrolled during the day with full-time students. Guilford College, for example, has a sizable evening program for residents of the area, while Hollins enrolls substantial numbers of older women in the same courses taken by their traditional students. In both cases, tuition charges for the older students are less expensive, based partly on the argument that the college does not have to provide extracurricular services for the adult students. The ability of a private college to develop a market for older students depends critically on the lack of supply of state-supported, low-tuition alternatives in the area. The ability to enroll adults in degree-credit courses, and charge a tuition high enough to produce net revenue for the college, is an opportunity that many colleges have pursued successfully in recent years.

Besides enrolling fewer minority students than desired, an imbalance in the number of men and women students, with women outnumbering men at several of the campuses, is occurring. Most colleges seek a fifty-fifty balance in male-female enrollments, but often enrollment is closer to 45 percent men, 55 percent or more women. Among the historically black colleges, Fisk, with nearly 75 percent women, is typical. One of the reasons many private colleges maintain the expensive sport of football is that it attracts male students who otherwise might enroll elsewhere.

It has been common for more than a decade to talk about the "missing middle class" in private colleges, and although that was mentioned occasionally, I did not encounter it as often or with as much passion as I had expected. Most of the colleges I visited are using their own unfunded student aid to help students from middle-income families enroll, and thus the issue may have been framed as a concern about the growth of such aid, rather than as a loss of middle-income students. The campuses I visited generally had 50 percent or more of their students on financial aid, many from middle-income families. The colleges have no alternative but to help middle-income students finance their education, for there are simply not enough full-pay students to meet the sector's enrollment goals.

Officials at several of the colleges expressed concerns about the quality of students enrolled, although there were nuances to the comments. One president indicated lack of satisfaction with the "intellectual toughness" of many of the students and hoped to instill greater rigor and discipline into the academic atmosphere on campus. The students, in this president's view, were of high quality but were a bit lazy and not sufficiently attuned to the critical use of the mind. On another campus, this concern took the form of worry that too many of the students were "laid back," more focused on extracurricular aspects of the college than on its primary academic mission. The belief on this campus is that recruiting materials have oversold the college's attractive location and associated life-style to the detriment of scholarly activities. An admissions officer at a third campus was concerned that the academic caliber of students being recruited by this college today was sharply lower than was true twenty-five years ago. By contrast, the presidents of two other colleges spoke enthusiastically about the commitment of students to volunteer work in the local community and beyond, clearly seeing service to others as a central part of the educational program. I suspect that a visitor to these or similar campuses at any time in this century would have encountered similar views—some dour, some upbeat—about the quality and nature of students currently enrolled. With one exception, my interviews did not reveal any sense of a fundamental decline in the quality of students enrolled today compared with earlier years, and when dissatisfaction was expressed, the issue seemed to be heightened aspirations for the college rather than a fall from grace.

The concept of enrollment management (a focus on recruitment, yield, and retention) seems well established at most of the colleges, even built into the administrative structure in some cases, such as Knox. The most clever idea that I encountered is at Wittenberg, where research has demonstrated that if a potential student does not rank Wittenberg as his or her first or second choice, the college rarely succeeds in enrolling that student, regardless of the effort put forth. To find out where the college ranks in the student's preferences, Wittenberg sends a postcard with the letter admitting the student, asking for the student's rank ordering of the colleges to which he or she has applied. (Because Wittenberg is on rolling admissions, these letters are sent throughout the admissions year, not all at once in April.) Virtually all of the students return this postcard survey, and the college concentrates further recruiting efforts on those for whom Wittenberg is a first or second choice, rather than on those for whom it is ranked lower. This simple postcard survey and the information it provides allows the college to concentrate follow-up efforts efficiently on those students who are likely to enroll.

In summary, then, the enrollment picture at these 12 colleges in 1992 is mixed, with over half not hitting their enrollment targets or achieving the desired diversity in the entering class. After several years of tuition increases outstripping income growth, concerns about overpricing for the market are much in evidence, contributing to a muting of tuition increases. For most private colleges, the future stretches ahead as one in which worry about meeting enrollment goals and earning sufficient net tuition revenue will be unrelenting. With the exception of a few golden years in past decades, however, this has been the fate of most private colleges throughout their existence. Much will depend on how the economy performs, but my site visits and related experience have not revealed a sense of despair or feeling of inevitable failure among those responsible for the welfare of private colleges.[3]

Management and Finance

The recession of the early 1990s was clearly being felt in several ways on the campuses, resulting in operating deficits at 9 of the 12 colleges in recent years. The deficits most commonly arose from unanticipated drops in enrollment coupled with sharp increases in student financial aid, resulting in less tuition revenue than budgeted. One response on several of the campuses has been staff reductions, through some combination of attrition, early retirement options, and elimination of positions. At Bowdoin, for example, as many as sixty staff and administrative positions may be cut over a three-year period as part of a multiyear plan to lower base operating costs. Many of these positions were added during the previous decade, when revenue growth was strong, and administrators do not believe that the quality of the college is threatened by this downsizing. Guilford College eliminated thirty-four staff and administrative positions in response to a potential $1.2 million operating deficit, a one-time cut that cannot be repeated without great damage to the quality of the institution. Other campuses are reducing staff in less dramatic numbers, usually through attrition rather than outright terminations. Cuts in faculty numbers are

3. See Michael S. McPherson and Morton Owen Schapiro, *Keeping College Affordable: Government and Educational Opportunity* (Brookings, 1991), chap. 6, for estimates of the sensitivity of college revenues to various economic scenarios.

less common, and where they are occurring, they are usually in part-time, non-tenure-track positions.

My sense, borne out by these 12 visits and other observations, is that except for the wealthiest schools, most private colleges have fairly little room to reduce costs substantially through staff reductions. Most liberal arts colleges have simply not had the revenue to expand staff in areas that can easily be scaled back without damaging the quality (or even the survival) of academic and extracurricular programs. On a small campus, productivity (or lack thereof) is visible and apparent to all, which tends to produce accountability directly. Most administrators at small colleges have an acute sense of how scarce financial resources are and how vital it is to generate maximum value from each dollar spent. Planned reduction in enrollment to reduce cost is also not a realistic option for most liberal arts colleges given their already small size. Thus, significant cost cutting, while a reasonable strategy for larger public and private universities, has much smaller potential as a solution to financial problems in the private college sector.

A second, short-run response to operating deficits is to increase the pay-out rate on endowments beyond a level that could prudently be maintained on a regular basis. In essence, this policy means drawing down unrestricted, quasi endowment (funds allocated to endowment by trustee action rather than by donor designation), which functions to some degree as an operating reserve. Drawing on quasi endowment is an action that few boards of trustees like to take, but as a one-time response to unexpected revenue shortfalls, such a decision is hardly catastrophic. In my experience, it is not uncommon for members of boards not to understand fully what quasi endowment is and how it can function as the institution's saving account, increased in good times and drawn on in hard times. Several of the colleges I visited, however, were operating under trustee-approved policies of multiyear operating deficits, funded by allocations from quasi endowment. Deficits of specific amounts had been approved, with a plan to eliminate them, typically over a three-year period, through a combination of increased revenues and cost reductions. Such policies are generally to be applauded as an improvement over a slavish focus on the annual operating budget, which represents only a portion of the institution's financial accounts.[4] A college can get into trouble, however, if the plan

4. Gordon Winston, "The Necessary Revolution in Financial Accounting," *Planning for Higher Education,* vol. 20 (Summer 1992), pp. 1–16.

for eliminating operating deficits is poorly conceived or based on wishful thinking.

Colleges also often try to balance their budgets when revenues fall by deferring maintenance of the physical plant. Few colleges incorporate capital costs adequately into their annual operating budgets,[5] and accounting for depreciation has only recently begun in response to pressure from the Financial Accounting Standards Board. (Most colleges take depreciation charges against the plant fund account, not the operating budget, so the effect of this change on institutional behavior is nil.) In my brief visits to the campuses, it was impossible to form any but the most fleeting impression of how much deferred maintenance was being accepted to cover imbalanced budgets.[6] In several instances, business officers stated that the college was clearly behind in upkeep, while in others, adequate funds were being spent for this purpose. (Dickinson College stands out as a beautifully maintained campus, with a well-conceived plan for keeping it that way.) The campus with the most severe problem that I visited was Fisk University, but an ingenious funding scheme including budget support from the federal Department of the Interior is under way, with nine buildings slated for thorough renovation.[7]

A further response to financial difficulties evident on several campuses is administrative reorganization, often coupled with more professional management of the business function. At Guilford College, for example, a new position of Provost was recently created, with all units of the college except development reporting directly there. In essence, the provost will function as a chief operating officer, freeing the president to devote more of his time to external relations and fundraising. At Knox, a dean of enrollment and institutional planning has been created, overseeing admissions, financial aid, and public relations. This position highlights the critical nature of enrollment, retention, and external visibility for this small, midwestern college. At Bowdoin, a new president has installed an entirely new administrative team with strong professional credentials in response to the judgment that the

5. Gordon Winston, "Why Are Capital Costs Ignored by Colleges and Universities, and What Are the Prospects for Change?" DP-14 (Williams College, July 1991).

6. Data on operation and maintence expense and on addition to plant for the 12 colleges are reported in chapter 6.

7. Federal support of building renovation at Fisk is discussed further in chapter 6.

college's financial problems were caused by weak management. Wittenberg University, among others, is experimenting with total quality management as a method to enhance productivity and institutional performance. Fisk University, perilously close to bankruptcy in 1983, is being dramatically turned around by the energetic and forceful leadership of Henry Ponder, president since 1984. Undeniably, visionary leadership and strong financial management can save small private colleges that are teetering on the brink of financial collapse.

In two instances, bad audit letters from accounting firms alerted the board and administration to weak financial procedures and prompted action to install better management controls. These campuses, for example, did not have encumbrance systems in place to account for funds committed but not yet spent, thereby weakening budgetary control. Surprisingly, considerable room remains in some colleges for reasonably straightforward management improvements that promise to give colleges greater control over their financial destinies.

But the central financial issue confronting these, and all, private colleges is the link between tuition, unfunded student aid, and enrollments, the subject of chapter 3. No one with whom I discussed these issues at the 12 colleges volunteered the analysis in that chapter as an explanation for institutional behavior, although several administrators did talk of comparing marginal revenue with marginal cost in making decisions about unfunded student aid, particularly when the alternative facing the college would have been an empty place in the entering class. The vice president for finance at Knox College did, however, describe an analysis similar to that in chapter 3. His approach is to convert head-count enrollments into FES—financial-equivalent students—a variation on the notion of FTE students. He divides gross tuition revenue by the tuition rate, which provides an enrollment number of full-pay students. By computing this measure each term, and comparing it to actual enrollments, he is able to track trends in a form closely related to net tuition revenue. He also converts the institutional financial accounts into the equivalent of what Gordon Winston has described as "global accounts," thereby focusing on changes in net wealth rather than just the operating budget.[8] In our conversation, it was clear that he had a good understanding of the importance of net tuition revenue and was not as concerned as many

8. Winston, "The Necessary Revolution."

business officers are by the degree to which tuition is being discounted at the college. (See table 5-3, where Knox College is seen to have a fairly aggressive rate of discounted tuition, as measured by beta.) The financial dilemma at Knox is that, even with an aggressive policy on unfunded student aid, total enrollment is still 100 to 150 students below what the college wants and could accommodate with current staff and facilities.

There is considerable concern on most campuses about the size and rate of growth of the unfunded student aid budget, and several of the campuses are attempting to cap such aid at some percentage of the educational and general budget. In some instances, including Bowdoin and Colorado College, such limitations had caused the college to abandon a pure need-blind admissions policy, a reasonable if uncomfortable response for colleges with sizable applicant pools.[9] Other colleges had attempted to limit such aid but were forced to relax the constraint when confronted with the profile of financial need represented in the applicant pool. Guilford College, for example, ran into financial difficulty when student financial need increased sharply in one year. They met the need but fell short of anticipated tuition revenue by more than $1 million, prompting difficult budget cuts elsewhere. Several other colleges had similar experiences in the early 1990s, rendering this issue one of the most worrisome to administrators and trustees. As discussed in chapter 3, the accounting treatment of student aid is not well designed for managerial decisionmaking. It is my hope that the discussion in chapter 3 will contribute to greater clarity in this critical area. As we enter an era in which annual tuition increases will be lower than in the 1980s, it is more than ever essential that administrators understand how net tuition revenue varies with changes in unfunded student aid.

In summary, colleges are pursuing several organizational and strategic changes designed to lower the rate of cost escalation, thereby helping to hold down the rate of future tuition increases. The search for increased revenue is focused mainly on development efforts. Although all but the most wealthy private colleges have limited ability to cut costs significantly, their autonomy and lack of bureaucratic structure give these colleges a nimbleness and ability to move quickly

9. See William G. Bowen and David W. Breneman, "Student Aid: Price Discount or Educational Investment," *Brookings Review*, vol. 11 (Winter 1993), pp. 28–31, for further discussion of the differing roles played by student aid.

and decisively in new directions, a source of real strength. Whatever their other problems, they are not the educational dinosaurs that many of the large public university systems have become.

Faculty

It does not require site visits to know that a central issue of concern to academic deans at liberal arts colleges is the supply of well-educated men and women eager to teach at such institutions for the salaries the colleges can afford. The prospect of labor market shortages of new Ph.D.'s in the late 1990s and early years of the next century has generated much discussion about the competitive position of various colleges and universities.[10] Small, private colleges are widely thought to be among those potentially at risk, for teaching loads are generally higher and salaries lower in these colleges than in public or private universities. The more far-sighted deans and presidents in colleges that can afford to do so have been working in recent years to raise salaries and enhance scholarly opportunities, especially for younger faculty, in anticipation of the need to be more competitive in the academic labor market.

Because potential shortages are not projected to occur until later in this decade, current experience may have limited value as an indicator of the attractiveness of liberal arts colleges to new faculty at that time. Nonetheless, of the 12 colleges, only Fisk has experienced any difficulty in recruiting desirable faculty members in several fields in recent years. Academic deans reported having large applicant pools for every position, and most were able to attract their first-choice candidate from within the pool. The only exceptions were at Fisk, where intense competition nationally for black faculty and relatively low salaries make recruiting in all fields difficult, and at Colorado College, where a uniform salary policy across all fields made it so difficult in the 1980s to recruit faculty in business administration that the major was eliminated.

As was true with student recruiting, recent financial problems at public universities have also contributed to the relative ease of faculty recruitment for private colleges. Several deans mentioned that candi-

10. William G. Bowen and Julie Ann Sosa, *Prospects for Faculty in the Arts and Sciences: A Study of Factors Affecting Demand and Supply* (Princeton University Press, 1989).

dates being interviewed reported that openings announced in public colleges and universities had been eliminated or the search discontinued midway through the recruiting season. The result was not only reduced competition for new faculty, but the appearance of greater stability and security in the private college sector. Should the financial picture improve for state universities as the decade progresses, this fairly recent feature of the labor market may rapidly disappear. Given the recent experience at these colleges, however, and uncertainties about projections of the future supply-demand balance for Ph.D.'s, it is not possible to argue with any certainty that private colleges are threatened by future faculty shortages.[11] Only time will tell.

Another factor that aids recruiting is that, as noted in chapter 1, the graduates of private colleges are represented among doctorate recipients in numbers disproportionate to their size. My experience at Kalamazoo College was echoed by several deans who observed that graduates of private colleges often want to return to teach in them. The educational experience these students received as undergraduates was of such high quality that they want the same environment for their teaching careers. While the professional values inculcated in most graduate programs work against careers in undergraduate teaching, the countervailing values embodied in a high-quality undergraduate experience can outweigh the emphasis placed in graduate school on research and university teaching. I am not able to quantify the size of this "undergraduate" effect, but those who interview candidates for college teaching positions can attest to its importance.

Although the supply of new faculty is not a current problem, several deans did express dismay at the narrowness of the professional training of new doctorates. A good college seeks breadth of intellectual interest in faculty, rather than the intense specialization that typifies doctoral education. While heartfelt, these concerns are hardly new, as anyone familiar with the history of graduate education and its critics is well aware. Rather than attempt to reform graduate education, the most sensible response for the liberal arts college is to encourage breadth of scholarly interest through curriculum, expectations for faculty development, and policies of promotion and tenure.

11. See Ronald G. Ehrenberg, "Academic Labor Supply," in Charles T. Clotfelter and others, *Economic Challenges in Higher Education* (University of Chicago Press, 1991), pp. 143–258, for analyses suggesting a less severe shortage problem than that projected by Bowen and Sosa.

In that regard, these 12 colleges differed significantly among themselves in teaching requirements and expectations of faculty scholarship. Teaching loads varied from a low of four courses a year at Bowdoin to eight at Olivet, with six courses a year most common. All of the deans want faculty to be productive scholars, but that expectation is stronger and built explicitly into the incentive system at colleges with lower teaching loads. What was interesting, however, was the breadth of definition given to scholarship; highly specialized books and refereed articles were only one form mentioned. Without exception, the deans seemed to support concepts of scholarship best described in the recent Carnegie Foundation volume, *Scholarship Reconsidered.*[12] Regardless of the quality or prestige of the college, the deans seemed willing to encourage and accept several forms of scholarly activity on the part of faculty. One dean summed up this view well by observing that he wanted evidence of intellectual activity, which could be expressed in many ways, including traditional scholarship, creation of new courses, professional work in the local community, or essays in magazines or newspapers.

Beginning at about the time of the 1985 conference on science in liberal arts colleges, held at Oberlin College, one began seeing references to "research colleges," usually the more prestigious and wealthy schools in this sector.[13] While no official association or organization of such colleges has been created, the idea is to single out a small group of colleges for designation as centers of serious research, comparable in quality if not in quantity to that produced by leading universities. Colleges seeking this identity typically lowered their teaching loads in recent years and increased expectations for faculty publication. One justification for this shift is the anticipated tightening of the academic labor market and the need to compete with universities for the best talent emerging from graduate schools. It is argued that one way to increase the attractiveness of liberal arts colleges is to mimic the working conditions of the university, with low teaching loads and excellent research facilities. Many people associated with liberal arts colleges share my view that this movement is troubling, for there seems to be little social value in transforming excellent colleges into miniature universities. The wide acceptance of a broad definition of scholarship

12. Ernest L. Boyer, *Scholarship Reconsidered: Priorities of the Professoriate* (Princeton, N.J.: Carnegie Foundation for the Advancement of Teaching, 1990).

13. See chapter 1 for details of the Oberlin conference.

that I encountered on my visits is an encouraging sign, pointing to a more sensible model for most colleges.[14]

Four of the colleges I visited had distinctive features for appointment and salary policies. Two of the colleges (Bradford and Olivet) do not grant tenure, having instead revolving term appointments, and two (Colorado College and Dickinson) have policies that constrain salaries to meet locally defined notions of equity. Colorado College seeks to minimize differences in faculty pay by discipline and does not allow any overlap of salaries among the professorial brackets, that is, the highest paid associate professor must earn less than the lowest paid full professor, and so forth. As noted earlier, this salary policy contributed to the decision to drop business administration as a major field of study because the college could not compete effectively for faculty in this relatively high salaried area. Dickinson College also does not have salary differentials by field and carries its communitarian values so far as to empower a faculty personnel committee to make recommendations on promotion, tenure, and salary for each member of the faculty. Whether such nonmarket values will serve these colleges well or poorly in more difficult labor market conditions is uncertain.

In sum, I encountered little sense of crisis or serious difficulty pertaining to faculty recruitment at these colleges. Most have some form of early retirement option in place to keep a flow of new positions open, a policy that allows the college to shift fields and hire younger, less expensive faculty. Except for officials at Fisk and Hollins, no one raised the issue of recruitment of women or of minority scholars as a concern, and I did not probe for such responses. With all of the national attention directed to diversity and multicultural programs, I assumed that such issues would be raised in our open-ended discussion of issues facing the colleges. Perhaps the fact that these matters did not arise should itself be seen as a cause for concern.

Academic Programs

The focus of my discussion about academic programs at these 12 campuses was limited primarily to new developments and new directions that were contemplated or under way. I did not review the current curriculum in any detail, nor the ebb and flow of courses; as any

14. This is a large and complicated topic, and full discussion of all the issues involved is beyond the scope of this book.

experienced observer knows, the catalog of course offerings imposes a broad, disciplinary structure within which courses are added and subtracted as the composition and interests of the faculty change. While new courses rarely prompt much serious debate (which is perhaps best explained by political log-rolling among faculty), new majors or changes in requirements often engage the faculty in strenuous and extended discussion. To the extent that an element of zero-sum competition is present when significant changes are proposed, the debate is usually an interesting mixture of genuine educational concern coupled with turf-protection from those who fear they will be potential losers in the competition for enrollments and resources. These forces tend, on balance, to inhibit change in the curriculum.

The programmatic development mentioned most often during my visits was an expansion of the international emphasis of the curriculum. The recent release of a report, *In the International Interest*, may have encouraged the interest of deans and presidents.[15] The report identified fifty-two private colleges selected by an ad hoc steering committee as demonstrating a strong commitment to international education and related programs. Five of the colleges that I visited (Bowdoin, Colorado College, Dickinson, Knox, and Union) were among those selected, on the basis of the following criteria:

—The percentage of undergraduate degrees awarded in international studies—foreign languages and areas studies (1986);

—The percentage of students studying abroad (1985, 1987);

—The percentage of alumni earning doctorates in modern languages (1977–86);

—The percentage of graduates entering the Peace Corps (1988); and

—The percentage of entering international students (1985).

The report describes the educational environment of these international liberal arts colleges as including an emphasis on language instruction, study-abroad programs, area studies, on-campus international programs and activities, and enrollment of international students. To varying degrees, these were the types of issues raised on my campus visits, especially at the five colleges included in the group but to a lesser extent at the others as well. The direct and obvious linkages of

15. David C. Engerman and Parker G. Marden, *In the International Interest: The Contributions and Needs of America's International Liberal Arts Colleges* (Beloit, Wisc.: International Liberal Arts Colleges, 1992).

an international emphasis to foreign language instruction and to social science and humanities fields make this direction of development a logical one for liberal arts colleges to pursue. By highlighting the connection of such programs to the global economy, an international focus helps to demonstrate the relevance of liberal education to potential students, their parents, and the local business community. I speak from personal experience, for Kalamazoo College has long had a strong international focus in its programs, both on and off campus.

At first glance, an emphasis on international education would seem to fit closely with the issue that has had the most explosive impact on the undergraduate curriculum in recent years—multiculturalism. In fact, however, these issues are quite different. While I am not aware of a definitive educational definition of multiculturalism, it clearly refers to groups in the United States whose experiences have been largely ignored by the traditional curriculum. *Change* magazine recently devoted an entire issue to multiculturalism, focused on ethnic and gender studies, including women's studies, African-American studies, Asian-American studies, Hispanic-American studies, Native-American studies, and gay and lesbian studies.[16] While there would seem to be obvious connections between international education and multiculturalism, in practice the two topics have led in different curricular directions. In my visits, virtually no one brought up ethnic and gender studies for discussion, and never in the context of international education. It is worth speculating briefly on why multicultural concerns are less in evidence on liberal arts campuses than in our larger institutions.[17]

Anyone who has followed campus discussions of gender and ethnic studies knows that, besides the intrinsic intellectual reasons for such work, an inherently political motivation is present. I do not use the word "political" in a pejorative sense but rather to acknowledge that including such studies in the curriculum is part of the struggle for recognition of those who have been relegated historically and economically to the margins of our society.[18] To succeed, political movements

16. "The Curriculum and Multiculturalism," special issue of *Change*, vol. 24 (January–February 1992). For the examples cited above, see the article in this issue by Arthur Levine and Jeanette Cureton, "The Quiet Revolution," pp. 25–29.

17. For survey evidence on this point, see Levine and Cureton, "The Quiet Revolution."

18. See the essays in Amy Gutmann, ed., *Multiculturalism and "The Politics of Recognition"* (Princeton University Press, 1992), for a similar treatment of this controversial issue.

require a critical mass of people of similar mind, and as data from earlier chapters indicate, the typical liberal arts college is limited in ethnic and racial diversity. With only a handful of African-American or Native-American students enrolled, it is not surprising that pressure to include such courses of study has been minimal. If my hypothesis is correct, then one would expect to find women's studies more fully developed at liberal arts colleges, a testable proposition.

The above discussion describes the academic issues I encountered most frequently on my visits. Other items of note were an emphasis on volunteer service (Westmont and Guilford), on the cocurriculum (Colorado College, Bradford), and on programs for older, part-time students living in the area (Hollins, Guilford). Other noteworthy items were unusual academic calendars (Colorado College's block plan), a strong and unusual specialty (Union's program in engineering, Olivet's program in insurance), a curriculum thoroughly revamped in the 1980s (the Bradford plan), the integration of Christian faith with learning (Westmont), and a striking art collection (the Stieglitz collection at Fisk).

Development

The function of institutional development (which typically includes, besides fund-raising, alumni relations, communications, and external relations) has increased in importance dramatically on most campuses, public as well as private, in recent years. Financial data in chapter 4 documented the degree to which liberal arts colleges depend on revenue raised annually, whether through annual fund contributions, capital gifts, bequests, or the various forms of deferred giving. Every college that I visited was actively engaged in efforts to increase the flow of dollars arriving through these channels.

One tends to think of fund-raising as having a long history in private colleges, and yet in several of the colleges visited, professionally conducted development efforts are of rather recent origin. At Bowdoin, for example, the development office is located in a former president's home on the edge of the campus, physically removed from the president's office and other parts of the campus. Prior presidents apparently did not look favorably on development, and its location reflects the marginal status accorded to it in the past. The vice president observed that Bowdoin has only had a fully professional development staff for about five years, suggesting that the college has considerable unrealized potential in fund-raising. Dickinson College, founded like Bowdoin in the eighteenth century, is also a fairly recent convert to development, with such efforts conducted by a fully professional staff for less than a decade. Although Dickinson has over 20,000 living alumni of record, the college's annual fund just surpassed the $1 million mark recently. That smaller and less well-known colleges have reached this level of annual giving suggests that Dickinson also has considerable unrealized potential for fund-raising. Indeed, many private colleges may not yet have tapped the resources potentially available to them, one reason for optimism about their future.

Every college I visited had just completed a capital campaign, was in the midst of a campaign, or was planning the next one. The dollar amounts of these actual or planned campaigns ranged from a low of $10 million to a high of $150 million (in that case, a lengthy campaign covering eight years in its public phase), with the modal campaign between $25 million and $40 million. Gifts from all sources at these colleges vary from slightly more than $1 million to approximately $10 million annually, with the modal amount between $3 million and $5 million. Presidents reported definite expectations in the college community on their role and performance in this aspect of the job, as well as the view that development will require ever-increasing presidential time in the years ahead. Not surprisingly, however, presidents at these colleges (as would be true of any set of institutions) differ in their skill and interest in fund-raising, and development officers were candid with me in expressing such judgments. In earlier years, a president who disliked fund-raising could spend little time doing it, but that is less true today. Tension between the president and the development staff is increasingly common as expectations rise, and I observed several instances of that problem during these visits.

Apart from such internal problems, development officers repeatedly mentioned three concerns. First, virtually all noted the growing competition for philanthropic support, especially from public colleges and universities now actively pursuing private gifts and grants. Second, several officials expressed concern that alumni and trustee support were lower than they should be, when compared with peer institutions. Third, several remarked that their college had failed to establish a well-defined or clear image with its various publics, implying that if the college were only better understood, greater support would be forthcoming.

With the possible exception of the growing competition for charitable funds from public colleges and universities, none of these concerns seems especially new or noteworthy. One suspects that a visitor ten, twenty, or even thirty years ago would have encountered similar comments. What is new is the emergence of a professional development office on liberal arts campuses, accompanied by informed judgments about the gift-giving performance of various constituencies. One would not have found a separate office, professionally staffed and devoted to fund-raising and external relations, at many colleges two or three decades ago. Instead, one might have found a director of church relations or of alumni relations, or an especially active trustee, who worked closely with the president on the tasks of development. Assuming that the campuses I visited are representative, then many colleges are still making the transition from an amateur to a professional development staff. This change, while not without its critics on campus, is essential if private colleges are to perform effectively in the instensely competitive market for charitable support.

Planning

Overall, some form of planning is being done at each campus, but I discovered no striking or original approaches to this task.

The term "strategic planning task force," or some derivative thereof, remains in vogue, with a composition and purpose unique to each campus. Planning is not built into the administrative structure of many small colleges, that is, few have an office of planning. Thus, the work that is done under that label typically involves an ad hoc assemblage of administrators and faculty (and occasionally students and trustees) who identify issues, collect data, interview members of the community, and issue a report. Some of the best planning is connected with a capital campaign, for such an effort requires a college to look at itself carefully, develop a list of needs, and set priorities among them. The campaign can be integrated with a multiyear budget, phasing in the expected flow of dollars with planned expenditures; in the college's literature, a campaign may be described as the mechanism for financing the strategic plan. Indeed, the fact that most private colleges have embraced the notion that they will always be in some stage of a campaign—planning, undertaking, completing, or preparing for the next one—may do more to produce continuous planning than any other force.

One of the original ideas behind strategic planning, as advocated by George Keller and others, was to look outward at the economic, social, and political environment in forming an understanding of where a college fits in an increasingly competitive environment and how it might position itself advantageously.[19] Several of the colleges were engaged in surveying students who had inquired about the college but who had not applied, or if accepted, had chosen not to enroll. This form of research into the student market, while not new, does give a college a better understanding of how it is perceived by potential students, which may lead to cosmetic or substantive changes. What is not clear from survey data of this type is how reliable student reports are on the role of price and financial aid; such surveys should be augmented with statistical analyses of actual demand behavior.

Surveys such as the above may be undertaken by consultants rather than the college's own staff. Another type of survey that can be conducted is a community assessment of educational needs of the older, place-bound population, and the ability and willingness to pay a significant tuition for degree-credit programs offered at night or on weekends. Bradford College, for example, has recently commissioned such a survey to determine whether a market exists for a nontraditional program, aimed at local residents who have community college credits and would like to earn a bachelor's degree. It was noted earlier that Hollins and Guilford are involved extensively in such programs, using regular and evening courses. Again, such efforts are hardly new but are still being explored by colleges as a further way to serve the community and earn additional revenue.

Another form of planning is internally focused, examining each part of the college and assessing its contribution to the mission of the institution. At Colorado College, for example, the president appointed a former dean and long-time faculty member to a newly created position of director of strategic planning. The new director visited

19. George Keller, *Academic Strategy: The Management Revolution in American Higher Education* (Johns Hopkins University Press, 1983); and Robert G. Cope, *Opportunity from Strength: Strategic Planning Clarified with Case Examples* (Washington: Association for the Study of Higher Education, 1987).

Yale, Dartmouth, and Wesleyan to learn what strategic planning was and concluded that at those institutions the term essentially meant downsizing and retrenchment. As implemented at Colorado College, the process has led to a careful look at the strengths and weaknesses of the distinctive curriculum known as the block plan, at the extensive cocurriculum developed in response to the college's unusual calendar, at the nature and quality of the students recruited, and at the desirable long-run size of the college. The president's departure in 1992 left the planning process suspended, for action would await the appointment of his successor. The relatively short term in office of many presidents (national average is six years) can pose a problem to the planning process, for a certain direction may be identified with the interests of the president, whose departure undercuts the plan.

Knox College was also in the middle of an unusual planning effort during my visit. A five-member strategic planning committee, composed entirely of faculty members, was engaged in a close look at the college, at what works and what does not. The committee interviewed faculty, key administrators, and all admissions staff to determine what they liked and disliked about Knox. Student opinions were sampled through questionnaires distributed in class. From this exercise, the committee has identified features of the college that are important to its members and areas that need strengthening. A new, more sharply defined mission statement is also likely to emerge from this process, for the committee found that admissions counselors, lacking a clear, official statement of what the college stands for, were largely making up their own definitions of the college. Underlying this concern may be the sense that at this point in its history, Knox needs strong, visionary leadership from key members of the administration. Detailed recommendations stemming from the committee's work were presented to the board of trustees at its June 1992 meeting. Interestingly, this exercise was delegated to faculty; on few campuses would one be likely to find administrators willing to cede such an important activity exclusively to a faculty committee.

I was at first surprised, and then intrigued, by the number of times administrators spoke of the lack of planning under the previous administration, with the college caught unprepared for enrollment decline, or without a strong development effort, or suffering from lax management and poor financial controls. It is hard to evaluate such comments because it is not uncommon for a college administrator privately to attribute various failings and deficiencies to a predecessor. I do not know whether this tendency is more pronounced in higher education than in other organizations, but if it is, the reason may be that new presidents are usually brought in from outside the institution rather than promoted from within. No current president would acknowledge a lack of thoughtful planning in his or her administration, but one suspects that an interviewer a decade hence would hear stories about the failure of the current leader to anticipate events and make the right decisions. In such instances, the truth may be unknowable.

Trustees

During the interviews I did not raise questions about trustees directly, so the only comments made were volunteered by the administrators themselves. One of the most dramatic transformations in a board of trustees occurred at Wittenberg in 1988, when the board was reduced from seventy-six to thirty-six members and became self-perpetuating. The larger board had been dominated by representatives of the Evangelical Lutheran Church, appointed by the church rather than by the board. The more manageable size of the board allows it to function more effectively and also gives Wittenberg an opportunity to develop greater gift-giving potential from its members. As one can imagine, a change of this magnitude was the end result of long and delicate negotiations, but the new board should help to strengthen Wittenberg in years to come.

If trustee relationships with the president sour, the result can be a disquieting sense of unease and uncertainty on the campus. Administrators feel that their actions are under scrutiny and may be questioned by the board; allegations of board interference in management are quick to follow. A feeling develops on campus that the board does not share the president's or the faculty's vision, and the campus is simply not able to reach agreement on direction and priorities. I encountered one instance where the above description applies, and no doubt a college does lose its sense of forward motion when trustee and administrative leadership is divided. Fortunately for the institution, the cure may be as simple as a change of presidency, especially when the new president arrives from outside, with no prior involvement in the controversies.

At another campus, trustees had urged a substantial restructuring of the roles and responsibilities of the top administrative positions to strengthen the internal management of the college and its fund-raising potential. Normally, one would expect such a change to arise from within the administration, but in this instance trustees were actively involved in assessing the needs and suggesting the direction of change. This case raises the question of whether the board had overstepped its bounds by moving from policy to management. That it happened, however, raises a more fundamental question about the role of boards of trustees. In the corporate world a trend toward more active involvement of outside directors is occurring as companies face demands for restructuring not easily accepted by management. Is increased activism also warranted in the nonprofit sector? Although this issue is far too large to deal with here, I would suggest that the parallel may be more apt for universities, particularly those with systemwide boards, than for private colleges. The difference is largely one of size and complexity, coupled with the earlier observation that most private colleges have relatively little capacity for significant downsizing and restructuring. The case above, then, should probably be seen more as an exception rather than the beginning of a trend.

The one other issue that came up at several campuses was the growing pressure from boards to slow tuition increase, following the rapid run-up of the 1980s. Approving the annual budget, including tuition rates, is a clear responsibility of the board, requiring serious analytical study and thorough debate. My interviews indicated that, in some instances, board members are balancing a concern for public opinion along with the financial needs of the college.

Government Policies

As noted at the beginning of this chapter, I arranged the eight categories into which most comments fell in roughly descending order based on the number of issues raised. It came as something of a surprise to realize after several visits that state and federal policies had rarely come up for discussion. In searching my notes, I could find virtually no comments about federal policy, even though the reauthorization of federal student aid programs was under way. Several interpretations are possible. Perhaps federal student aid programs are viewed as part of the general background and as such warrant little explicit comment. Presidents may feel they have little ability to affect the outcome of federal debates and thus spend little time thinking about them. Perhaps, at the time of my visit, the federal budget deficit, coupled with a Republican administration not seen as supportive, precluded any new or striking initiatives. But underlying all these plausible explanations, I sensed a fundamental shift from the view that obtained in the 1960s and 1970s, when higher education leaders looked to Washington for support and new programs. Administrators in the early 1990s conveyed a sense that the destiny of their colleges would be worked out, for good or ill, with resources available within the institutional family. Federal grant and loan programs remain vitally important, but that is not where the action was in 1992 for most college officials, if my interviews were representative.

State policies and programs for student aid, however, were mentioned in several interviews. The president of Union College in New York was outraged by the recent cuts sought by the Cuomo administration in both the so-called Bundy aid and in TAP—the tuition assistance program. The day before my visit he had delivered a strong public speech, condemning the administration for ignoring the needs of students and colleges in New York's private sector. State student aid policies, and concern about reduced appropriations, also came up in my visits at Knox College (Illinois), Guilford (North Carolina), and Westmont (California). Presidents may feel more directly involved in programs in their own states as opposed to those emanating from Washington; an individual may be able to affect the outcome of budget debates closer to home. But their concerns also reflect the importance of state programs for students attending private colleges; any slippage in public support for such programs is seen as a threat, politically and financially.

I judge it a sign of strength and encouragement that presidents do not see the salvation of their colleges depending on increased support from state or federal governments. The advances that were made in state and federal student aid programs in the 1960s and 1970s were and are vitally important, and any sharp drop in support from these sources would damage most private colleges. But it is unlikely that governmental support will increase by much in the foreseeable future, and presidents seem realistic about those prospects. I suspect many would agree that the most important thing the federal government can do for higher education is help the economy achieve increased growth and productivity.

CHAPTER SIX

The Future

As NOTED earlier, the 1980s began with a spate of pessimistic forecasts and projections about the economic problems facing all of higher education, especially private colleges.[1] Most analysts projected enrollments to decline between 5 percent and 15 percent, and fears were expressed that private colleges and universities would suffer severely if the tuition gap between public and private institutions continued to increase. Making matters worse, the economy was mired in high unemployment and high inflation, and few observers foresaw an end to these conditions of "stagflation." Instead, the decade turned out very differently. Inflation was tamed, the stock market boomed, college enrollments increased, and private colleges and universities held their market share, even though private tuitions soared at rates no one imagined or thought possible. Whatever hubris the analytic community had at the decade's start, little remained at the decade's end.

Apart from dramatic changes in the economy, four factors of importance were unanticipated by those writing in the late 1970s. First, few economists foresaw the sharp turnaround in the relative value of high school versus college education in the labor market. Growing forces of global competition, poorly understood or foreseen in the 1970s, laid waste to high-wage manufacturing jobs for high school graduates, abruptly reversing the 1970s pattern of a declining rate of return to college. Second, the college-pricing strategy of sharp increases in tuition coupled with increased discounting, discussed at length in chapter 3, was not foreseen or even imagined as a viable policy in the 1970s, even though its roots lay in the inflation and slow economic growth of that period. Third, the increased emphasis on quality,

---

1. This literature is discussed in chapter 2.

prestige, and marketing of colleges introduced a new way of thinking and operating on campus, characterized by Gordon Winston as an increase in maximizing behavior.[2] Fourth, the ability and willingness of undergraduate colleges to shift curricular emphasis toward professional programs, and the apparent success of that survival strategy, was not foreseen by those who predicted massive closures of small colleges in the 1980s and beyond (see appendix A). Each of these events should be humbling to would-be prognosticators.

Quite apart from the inability to foresee major shifts in the economy and in the behavior of institutions, the lack of timely data also hinders analytic efforts. That the financial data used in this study are nearly four years old is an unfortunate commentary on the inadequate resources devoted to data collection, rendering the analyst essentially an historian. In this study, for example, available data do not cover recent years of recession, in which the fortunes of private colleges may well have taken a sharp downturn. In normal times (whatever they may be), the pace of change in higher education tends to be glacial, and being two or three years behind in the data is not harmful; when the economy is shifting as rapidly as it has in recent years, however, this delay leads to a serious lack of knowledge and a diminished ability to respond in a timely fashion.

Finally, our modest knowledge of the relationships connecting higher education and the economy, and the lack of well-tested theories of behavior in nonprofit institutions, limits the ability to forecast. Recent work is extending the understanding of these areas of inquiry, and this book is intended as a contribution to that effort.[3] The serious research devoted to the economic behavior of colleges and universities, and the effect of the economy on them, remains minuscule, however, and thus forecasting efforts do not have a solid base of knowledge on which to build.

On one matter, however, all recent work would agree, and that is the central importance of the economy relative to all other factors in

2. Gordon C. Winston, "Hostility, Maximization, and the Public Trust," *Change*, vol. 24 (July–August 1992), pp. 20–27.

3. See Charles T. Clotfelter and others, *Economic Challenges in Higher Education* (University of Chicago Press, 1991); Stephen A. Hoenack and Eileen L. Collins, eds., *The Economics of American Universities: Management, Operations, and Fiscal Environment* (State University of New York Press, 1990); and Michael S. McPherson and Morton Owen Schapiro, *Keeping College Affordable: Government and Educational Opportunity* (Brookings, 1991).

determining the fate of higher education. The financial circumstances of private colleges in the 1990s and beyond will be especially sensitive to changes in the growth and distribution of family incomes and to the job security that families feel; to trends in stock market and other asset values; to changing labor market demands for graduates and the skills rewarded; to the cost and availability of student loans; and to state and federal policies governing grant support for students. Any serious attempt to forecast the future of liberal arts colleges would have to consider each of these forces. A strong and growing economy, however, would do more to ensure the future of private colleges than any new program or policy of government.

Prospects for Twelve Colleges

Although no forecasts are made for the liberal arts college sector, it does seem reasonable to comment briefly on the prospects that face the 12 colleges visited as part of this study. As a part of that effort, tables 6-1 and 6-2 provide data from the Williams College data set for the 12 schools, in the same format used in chapter 4.[4] The vignettes for each college will draw on these data as well as on the site-visit findings.

Bowdoin

This well-known college, which will celebrate its 200th anniversary in 1994, should also have cause at that time to celebrate much-needed and long-overdue management improvements. Data in tables 6-1 and 6-2 confirm the existence of operating deficits through the 1980s, culminating in a $2.5 million deficit in a $44 million budget in 1989–90. Net revenue per student was less than net spending in 1979 and 1989, despite a substantial increase of 6.1 percent a year in net revenue over that decade. The sharp annual increase in gifts and endowment revenue of 9.6 percent may have produced a false sense of security during the 1980s, for the college increased spending at the relatively high rate of 5.3 percent a year. Among the categories of expenditure, student services grew exceptionally at 12 percent annually.

4. In the discussion that follows, reference is also made to data in tables 5-1 through 5-4.

Bowdoin is a strong college academically, with a sizable applicant pool (3,242 applied in 1991), high selectivity (27 percent admitted), and a strong yield (47 percent enrolled). Despite sharply rising revenue, the college simply was living beyond its means during the past decade, having reached a total staff of 630 for an enrollment of 1,350 at the end of the 1980s. Comparing outlays for institutional support (general administrative expense) at Bowdoin with the other colleges in table 6-2 shows just how far out of line Bowdoin had become by 1989; at $5,940 a student, this expense is roughly twice that of any of the other 11 colleges. Robert Edwards, who became president in 1990, has replaced all senior administrators and is reducing staff positions by approximately sixty over a three-year period, which should restore financial balance. Bowdoin is a prime example of a college experiencing managerial drift during the 1980s, a pattern that could not be continued. Under its new leadership, Bowdoin's prospects are excellent.

Colorado College

Considerable uncertainty about future direction was evident during my visit to this college, for Gresham Riley, president since 1981, had recently announced that he would be stepping down from that position. A new planning effort was thus effectively on hold, awaiting appointment of a new president in 1993. Several administrators expressed concern that the board and the campus were not fully united in a common vision, further adding to the uncertainty. Nonetheless, this is a strong college, as the financial data in tables 6-1 and 6-2 suggest. Net revenue grew at 6.7 percent a year during the 1980s, while net spending increased by 4.5 percent. Spending increases were distributed fairly evenly among the various categories of expenditure, and although unfunded student aid grew by 10.6 percent annually, net tuition and fees increased by 3.7 percent a year, while gifts and endowment grew by 9.6 percent annually. In 1991, 2,770 students applied, 50 percent were accepted, and 36 percent enrolled, all strong figures. Aspirations of faculty and administrators at the college are high, for they seek to move the college to the next level of excellence and national prominence. (One of the sources of strain is the fear that the board of trustees may not share this vision.) The incoming president, Kathryn Mohrman, will need to unite all members of the college community behind a shared vision. The prospects for Colorado College are excellent.

Table 6-1. *Selected Revenue Items, Twelve Site-Visit Colleges, 1979–89*[a]
Constant 1990–91 dollars unless noted otherwise

| | College | | | | | | | | | | | |
Item	Bowdoin	Colorado	Union	Dickinson	Hollins	Wittenberg	Knox	Bradford	Guilford	Westmont	Fisk	Olivet
Net revenue												
1979	12,629	10,935	12,830	11,408	11,501	8,169	n.a.	11,210	n.a.	7,871	11,629	7,949
1989	22,892	20,869	20,982	20,415	17,087	11,551	15,151	12,888	12,318	12,415	12,516	10,510
Percent change	6.10	6.70	5.10	6.00	4.00	3.50	...	1.40	...	4.70	0.70	2.80
Net tuition and fees												
1979	6,982	6,231	7,341	7,491	7,054	5,634	6,994	5,239	4,003	5,539	4,185	4,881
1989	10,172	8,987	10,559	10,949	8,226	7,715	7,301	5,813	5,847	7,332	4,220	5,187
Percent change	3.80	3.70	3.70	3.90	1.50	3.20	0.40	1.00	3.90	2.80	0.10	0.60
Gifts and endowments												
1979	4,900	4,644	4,699	3,730	3,753	1,889	n.a.	5,866	n.a.	1,933	4,815	2,877
1989	12,214	11,613	9,777	9,150	8,216	3,194	7,264	6,418	5,648	4,912	5,044	4,928
Percent change	9.60	9.60	7.60	9.40	8.20	5.40	...	0.90	...	9.80	0.50	5.50
Federal grants and contracts												
1979	747	60	279	48	454	416	249	105	33	399	2,596	16
1989	506	151	134	168	170	229	426	148	92	171	3,252	320
Percent change	-3.80	9.70	-7.10	13.30	-9.40	-5.80	5.50	3.50	10.80	-8.10	2.30	34.90

Gross tuition and fees											
1979	9,233	7,373	8,564	8,259	8,275	7,228	8,083	6,697	5,385	6,698	5,035	6,177
1989	13,864	11,660	12,845	13,501	10,083	11,526	10,548	9,153	7,924	8,933	5,081	6,354
Percent change	4.10	4.70	4.10	5.00	2.00	4.80	2.70	3.20	3.90	2.90	0.10	0.30
Total scholarship aid from institutional funds											
1979	2,251	1,142	1,222	768	1,221	1,594	1,089	1,458	1,382	1,159	851	1,295
1989	3,691	2,672	2,286	2,552	1,857	3,810	3,247	3,340	2,076	1,600	861	1,167
Percent change	5.10	8.90	6.50	12.80	4.30	9.10	11.50	8.60	4.20	3.30	0.10	−10.00
Pell and SEOG grants											
1979	369	246	220	203	249	226	311	423	295	294	1,552	724
1989	351	296	243	239	246	281	506	416	278	277	1,375	920
Percent change	−0.50	1.90	1.00	1.60	−0.10	2.20	5.00	−0.20	−0.60	−0.60	−1.20	2.40

Source: Williams College Project on the Economics of Higher Education. See appendix B.
n.a. Not available.
a. Calculated per full-time-equivalent (FTE) student. Percent changes are annual averages.

Table 6-2. *Selected Expenditure Items, Twelve Site-Visit Colleges, 1979–89*[a]
Constant 1990–91 dollars unless noted otherwise

Item	College											
	Bowdoin	Colorado	Union	Dickinson	Hollins	Wittenberg	Knox	Bradford	Guilford	Westmont	Fisk	Olivet
Net spending												
1979	14,370	9,138	10,668	9,815	11,051	8,359	11,274	10,721	6,150	8,053	11,008	7,570
1989	24,693	14,203	15,921	13,630	13,343	10,321	12,137	15,589	8,871	10,503	11,528	7,879
Percent change	5.30	4.50	4.10	3.30	1.90	2.10	0.70	3.80	3.70	2.70	0.50	0.40
Instruction, self-supported research												
1979	4,183	4,536	4,323	4,731	4,807	3,427	5,109	2,874	3,309	2,858	3,458	3,048
1989	8,016	6,206	6,997	5,465	6,339	4,476	5,144	5,122	4,124	4,160	3,925	2,427
Percent change	6.70	3.20	4.90	1.50	2.80	2.70	0.10	5.90	2.20	3.80	1.30	-2.30
Academic support												
1979	1,152	354	147	288	223	595	58	n.a.	n.a.	n.a.	348	56
1989	1,381	541	505	604	513	764	162	319	n.a.	627	395	n.a.
Percent change	1.80	4.30	13.10	7.70	8.70	2.50	10.80	...	...	...	1.30	...
Library												
1979	902	481	509	557	545	369	460	489	306	437	421	359
1989	1,305	614	681	813	609	n.a.	562	563	484	n.a.	450	339
Percent change	3.80	2.50	3.00	3.90	1.10	...	2.00	1.40	4.70	...	0.70	-0.60
Student services												
1979	1,091	1,295	944	733	1,004	1,009	1,092	2,018	940	796	1,673	792
1989	3,395	2,410	1,431	1,602	1,654	1,391	1,591	2,689	1,654	1,327	1,343	1,174
Percent change	12.00	6.40	4.20	8.10	5.10	3.30	3.80	2.90	5.80	5.20	-2.20	4.00

Institutional support												
1979	4,487	1,204	2,884	1,591	2,485	1,233	2,397	1,743	1,045	2,873	2,961	1,555
1989	5,940	2,703	2,985	2,171	2,277	1,998	2,906	2,872	1,569	2,568	2,553	3,046
Percent change	2.80	8.40	0.30	3.20	−0.90	4.90	1.90	5.10	4.10	−1.10	−1.50	7.00
Operation and maintenance												
1979	2,449	1,205	1,167	1,416	1,047	1,658	1,406	2,682	468	935	1,612	1,521
1989	3,872	1,634	1,551	1,520	1,611	1,321	1,160	2,238	936	1,797	1,344	893
Percent change	4.70	3.10	2.90	0.70	4.40	−2.20	−1.90	−1.80	7.20	6.80	−1.80	−5.20
Scholarships, unrestricted												
1979	644	464	794	480	480	782	163	931	394	808	797	905
1989	958	1,272	1,695	2,017	1,611	2,833	2,427	1,717	907	1,499	376	1,052
Percent change	4.10	10.60	7.90	15.40	12.90	13.70	31.00	6.30	8.70	6.40	−7.20	1.50
Scholarships, restricted												
1979	1,976	923	649	491	991	1,038	1,237	949	1,282	646	1,606	1,114
1989	3,085	1,697	834	773	1,005	1,259	1,326	2,039	1,447	376	1,859	1,034
Percent change	4.60	6.30	2.50	4.60	0.10	1.90	0.70	7.90	1.20	−5.30	1.50	−0.70
Plant additions												
1979	924	1,411	1,383	1,685	674	1,829	1,570	n.a.	322	73	n.a.	104
1989	1,299	2,579	1,796	3,549	3,430	2,478	1,285	771	2,796	1,209	144	1,083
Percent change	3.50	6.20	2.60	7.70	17.70	3.10	−2.00	. . .	24.10	32.40	. . .	26.40

Source: See table 6-1.
n.a. Not available.
a. Calculated per FTE student. Percent changes are annual averages.

Union

Another venerable institution, Union College, will celebrate its 200th anniversary in 1995. Union is one of a small number of liberal arts colleges to have an undergraduate program in engineering, complementing its strong programs in the natural sciences. Several administrators commented that the presence of an engineering program may cloud the image of the college, for it gives Union a look and feel different from other high-quality liberal arts colleges. In any event, Union had 2,752 applicants in 1991, accepted 52 percent, and enrolled 31 percent; strong numbers, although the yield rate is on the low side, indicating that the college does lose many of those it seeks to enroll. Financial data in tables 6-1 and 6-2 demonstrate strength, with net revenue up 5.1 percent a year over the decade, while spending increased at 4.1 percent annually. Comparison of the spending figures with Bowdoin, for example, highlights differences between these two colleges; per student outlays at Union for academic support, library, student services, institutional support, and operation and maintenance of physical plant are sharply lower than at Bowdoin. Bowdoin failed to control its expenses for much of the decade, and using Union as an index, that fact is driven home. Roger Hull, president since 1990, can be expected to move aggressively on the fund-raising front and is strongly promoting international education at the college. Under his leadership, prospects at Union are excellent.

Dickinson

Founded in 1773, Dickinson is a beautifully maintained campus, with buildings made of limestone from its own quarry. For a college of its age and distinction, the most surprising fact is the relatively low value of its endowment, $63.5 million in fiscal 1991. Apparently, presidents prior to the incumbent, Lee Fritschler, and his predecessor, Sam Banks, did not participate actively in fund-raising, not seeing that as an important part of the job. As a result, considerable potential seems to exist for increasing the flow of gifts to endowment, although the opportunity lost in earlier years can never be made up. The financial figures in tables 6-1 and 6-2 are strong, with net revenue up 6 percent a year over the 1980s, while net spending grew at only 3.3 percent a year. Net tuition revenue grew at a healthy 3.9 percent a year, while gifts and endowment increased at a substantial 9.4 percent annually. Expenses were generally held in check, although unfunded student aid did increase at 15.4 percent annually, a relatively high rate, indicative of Dickinson's competitive position. In 1991, 3,639 students applied, 66 percent were admitted, and 23 percent enrolled—Dickinson obviously faces tough competition for students. The college has invested heavily in international education and has particularly strong programs for language and area studies, complete with many high-technology communication facilities. With proper attention devoted to fund-raising, the prospects for Dickinson are excellent.

Hollins

As the only women's college visited, the interpretation of the status of Hollins has potential relevance beyond its campus, extending to the remaining 84 colleges in this category. As already noted, women's colleges as a group seem to be doing as well as (or better than) the average liberal arts college, and the data for Hollins support that judgment. Net revenue increased at 4 percent annually, while net spending grew at 1.9 percent; net tuition gained only 1.5 percent annually, but gifts and endowment increased at a substantial 8.2 percent a year. Spending was kept in check, and general administrative expense (institutional support) declined in real terms, down 0.9 percent a year. Unfunded student aid was up 12.9 percent annually, a high rate of increase but hardly unprecedented. Only 685 women applied in 1991, however, down from 857 in 1989 and 850 in 1983; 82 percent were admitted in 1991, and 40 percent enrolled. And here lies the dilemma for most women's colleges—enrollment. The problem is not one of diminished quality of academic programs or reduced attractiveness of campus facilities; the problem for many women's colleges lies in the changing values of young women and in the shortcomings of extracurricular life. As men's colleges have adopted coeducation, women's colleges have lost single-sex companion schools for social events; this loss occurred for Hollins when Washington and Lee, a neighboring college, began admitting women in 1985. On weekends, women's colleges are often abandoned, as students seek social engagements elsewhere. As the number of young women interested in single-sex colleges declines, women's colleges are put in the difficult position of needing to explore alternatives, such as coeducation, but have difficulty holding that discussion publicly, especially after the highly visible uproar that accompanied that proposal at Mills College in California. Hollins last seriously considered (and rejected) coeducation in 1971, when many women's colleges examined that option, but the subject has since been off-limits. Margaret O'Brien, the new and energetic young president, spoke out on the subject early in her first year and encountered a backlash that ended further public conversation. The college is committed to remaining single sex, but not to the point where low enrollments would threaten academic quality or financial viability. If enrollments have not increased significantly in five years, the issue will probably be revived for serious consideration.[5] Given this big imponderable, the prospects for Hollins remaining a college for women only must be rated uncertain.

Wittenberg

Wittenberg is an institution with far less wealth than those considered thus far; table 6-1 shows that net revenue per student in 1989 ($11,551) was lower than any of the other 11 colleges except Fisk. As a result, net spending per student in 1989 ($10,321), was also among the lowest in the group.[6] Nonetheless, Wittenberg was in a balanced financial position in 1989, with net revenues exceeding net spending, the former having grown at a faster rate than the latter over the decade. Despite a high growth rate of unfunded student aid (up 13.7 percent a year), net tuition revenue increased at 3.2 percent annually, about average for all colleges. (Note in table 5-3, chapter 5, that the value of beta—unfunded aid divided by gross tuition revenue—had reached 25 percent at Wittenberg in 1989.) Of the 12 site-visit colleges, the contribution of gifts and endowment per student to net revenue at Wittenberg ($3,194 in 1989) was the lowest figure recorded. Fund-raising has clearly not been a strength of this school historically, a situation that needs to change. One area in which short-term savings were realized was

5. Current enrollment at Hollins of traditional, full-time students is 825; I was told that the ideal enrollment would be 1,200, while a realistic goal would be 1,000 students.
6. Regional cost differences may result in a smaller difference in real resources per student than the dollar figures indicate.

operation and maintenance of plant, where spending declined by 2.2 percent a year over the decade.

Wittenberg's strength lies in its strong and effective admissions office, which has managed, in the words of the dean, to "bend the trend" in these years of demographic decline. In 1991, 2,418 students applied (a high figure for midwestern colleges), 77 percent were accepted, and 34 percent enrolled. Because Ohio has many excellent private colleges, Wittenberg operates in an intensely competitive market for students but has managed to maintain enrollments at or near the desired level. If it can continue to enroll 600 or more new students a year (a large number relative to most colleges), and improve its fundraising efforts, the prospects for Wittenberg will be good.

Knox

This fine midwestern college has struggled with enrollment for much of the past decade, running about 150 students below the level that would make sense economically and educationally for the college. In 1991, 1,029 students were enrolled, while the college could accommodate 1,200 with its current physical plant and faculty. Colleges in the Midwest face difficult competition from public universities—particularly flagship campuses—that combine high prestige with low tuition. The best private colleges in Michigan compete with the University of Michigan, Ann Arbor, which enjoys enormous prestige and standing within the state, while Knox must compete with the equally well-regarded University of Illinois at Champaign/Urbana. Midwestern colleges also have difficulty recruiting students from the populous eastern states, where a predisposition toward private higher education exists, because of distance and the large number of high-quality private colleges in the East. As a result, midwestern colleges of high quality struggle incessantly with the problem of smaller applicant pools and stronger public-sector competition than do their peers in the east. In 1991, for example, Knox received only 796 applications, admitted 78 percent, and enrolled 36 percent. Maintaining enrollment is not a new problem for midwestern colleges, but it is enervating to worry each and every year about making the class.

One result of this struggle for students was the sharp increase in institutionally funded scholarships, the dollar value growing from $1,089 a student in 1979 to $3,247 in 1989, a growth rate of 11.5 percent a year.[7] As a consequence, net tuition revenue increased by only 0.4 percent a year (table 6-1), and Knox was forced to keep net spending down to a minimal annual growth of 0.7 percent. Outlays for instruction were virtually unchanged in real terms over the decade, while spending on plant maintenance declined nearly 2 percent a year. These numbers reflect a grinding reality of life in many midwestern colleges, and there is no obvious quick fix. State policies are critically important to colleges of high quality caught in this difficult competitive situation, squeezed by prestigious, low-tuition public institutions and declining numbers of high school graduates. Perhaps the best hope is that high school graduates are projected to increase in the latter half of this decade, which may enable Knox to reach a financially stronger enrollment level of 1,150 to 1,200 students. If colleges of the quality of Knox should falter, Illinois and the nation would truly be the poorer. Prospects for Knox have to be rated as guardedly optimistic.

Bradford

This small college in Massachusetts (enrollment of 475 in 1991) received considerable national attention during the 1980s as then-president Arthur Levine implemented a new and innovative curriculum known as the Bradford plan.[8] There is little doubt among those on the campus that this new plan, and the publicity that the college received as a result, saved the school from probable collapse. Financial problems continue to plague the college, however, as data in tables 6-1 and 6-2 and my site-visit interviews indicate. Net spending simply increased at a much faster rate (3.8 percent a year) over the decade than did net revenue (1.4 percent annual gain), resulting in a growing gap between income and expense. The college is currently operating under a three-year plan to phase out operating deficits, largely through enrollment increases. During the past decade, revenue from net tuition and from gifts and endowments grew modestly, 1.0 and 0.9 percent a year, respectively. Spending on instruction was up 5.9 percent annually,

7. The increase in beta in table 5-3, chapter 5, also captures this trend, as the ratio of unfunded aid to gross tuition revenue jumped from 1 percent in 1978 to 23 percent in 1989.

8. Janice S. Green, "Planning at a Small Institution: Bradford College," *New Directions for Institutional Research*, no. 67 (Fall 1990), pp. 39–54.

while general administration (institutional support) grew by 5.1 percent a year; unfunded student aid, however, was held to an annual increase of only 6.3 percent.

To a considerable degree, Bradford's dilemma is that of most colleges with such small enrollments—the college cannot achieve economies of scale operating with so few students. A rough rule of thumb often mentioned in discussions of small colleges is that financial problems intensify when enrollment falls below 1,000 students—there are simply too few students to carry the necessary overhead costs. Barring some extraordinary infusion of endowment, Bradford's future will hinge on its ability to increase enrollments. Prospects for this college, its excellent and innovative curriculum notwithstanding, would have to be rated uncertain.

Guilford

Recent experience at this Quaker college exemplifies the problem caused by lack of timely financial data from national sources. The numbers in tables 6-1 and 6-2 show that the college was faring reasonably well financially through 1989; net revenue exceeded net spending significantly in 1989, net tuition revenue grew by nearly 4 percent a year over the decade, and student aid from institutional sources rose by a relatively modest 4.2 percent annually. Additions to physical plant were up sharply (24.1 percent annually), but that figure, in and of itself, need not be a cause for concern. The site visit, however, revealed that the college had been faced with a potential operating deficit of $1.2 million, caused by a sudden and unexpected increase in student financial need, which the college met with unfunded aid. Because Guilford has a small endowment ($26 million), it had little cushion with which to cover this unexpected drop in net tuition revenue. In response, a substantial downsizing of thirty-four staff positions was undertaken, and the president has been urged to spend much more time fundraising. A palpable sense of nervousness pervaded the campus in 1992, prompted by the reduction in staff and related uncertainty.

Guilford is a college with a strong sense of community and an ethos of service. The president, William Rogers, believes strongly that the education offered makes a moral difference in the lives of students and in their subsequent contributions to society. Because many graduates have entered relatively low-paying occupations, gift-giving potential of alumni is not large, nor does the college have many prospects for sizable gifts. A state program of student aid provides $1,150 on a non-need basis for North Carolina residents, but that covers only about one-third of the student body. North Carolina has a strong system of public higher education and a tradition of low public tuition, adding to the competitive problems of private colleges in the state. Officials were uncertain what further steps the college would take if student financial need continued to grow. As was true for Knox College, it would be a serious loss to the region if Guilford should falter. Renewed emphasis on fund-raising, coupled with tighter management controls and the intangible assets that small colleges can draw on in times of adversity, prompt a guardedly optimistic judgment about the prospects of this college.

Westmont

A fairly new college, Westmont was founded in 1940 and was originally located in Pasadena but moved to the grounds of a large estate overlooking Santa Barbara in 1945. Westmont is an evangelical Christian college but is not affiliated with any denomination, similar to Wheaton College in Illinois and Gordon College in Massachusetts. The college stresses the integration of faith and learning, and faculty members are required to sign a statement of faith. George Blanken-baker, the academic dean, indicated that Westmont is more liberal theologically than most of its peers in the Christian College Coalition, a membership association of approximately eight-five colleges located in Washington, D.C.

Because it is located in an expensive residential area, Westmont must contend with several unique problems. The college operates under a conditional use permit granted by the county that puts strict limits on total enrollment, number of cars, sound levels of stereo equipment in dormitories, and related provisions. So strict is this enrollment limit, that in 1987, when enrollments hit 1,217 (the limit at that time was 1,200), the college had to offer financial incentives to encourage a small number of students to enroll elsewhere for a semes-ter—twenty-seven students accepted the offer, keeping the college within its size limit. Following extensive negotiation, a new absolute limit of 1,235 students a semester was adopted, linked by a complicated formula to a moving enrollment average. The student body currently numbers only 1,115, taking the enrollment cap out of play, but causing financial difficulties for the college.

Data in tables 6-1 and 6-2 paint a picture of a financially healthy college in 1989, but once again, intervening years have clouded the picture. The recent recession has taken a hard toll on California, and Westmont has suffered, along with most of the state's private and public colleges and universities. Officials attribute the enrollment drop to the recession, as nervous families turn away from higher-priced colleges in favor of public universities, in and out of state. Student financial need has risen sharply, and the college is hard-pressed to meet that need, particularly as the level of Cal grants (the state student aid program) has not kept pace with rising costs. (In 1976, the maximum Cal grant covered Westmont's tuition, but now it covers less than half.) Ironically, students at state universities are drawing more Cal grant funds, as fees in the public sector have risen sharply.

Westmont recruits in an unusual way, relying heavily on advertisements in such magazines as *Campus Life, Christianity Today*, and *Parents and Teenagers*. The college also recruits through such groups as Young Life and the Campus Crusade for Christ. They do not buy search labels from the College Board, as most colleges do. The one bright spot caused by the state's budget problems is that the enrollment caps and other problems in state colleges and universities prompted an increase in applications to Westmont and other private colleges in 1992. It was not clear at the time of my visit how many would actually enroll, however, because of limited grant aid. Given the uncertainty about the future of California's economy, and its impact on enrollment, state support for student aid, and the climate for fund-raising, president David Winter expressed a view of cautious optimism about prospects for the college. His judgment seems accurate.

Fisk

The recent story of this institution is nothing short of amazing, for a college that was effectively bankrupt in 1983, with utilities shut off for nonpayment of bills, is currently on its way to recovery. Fisk is an important institution historically in U.S. higher education, having been founded at the close of the Civil War for the following purposes: to provide quality education for all people, regardless of race, creed, or color, and to provide liberal education of a quality set by standards of American higher education, not "Negro" education. In its early years, the college had to rely on concerts by its Jubilee Singers to raise funds for building construction; the oldest building on campus, Jubilee Hall, was financed in this fashion. Fisk has always been distinctive among historically black colleges, for it has never deviated from its mission of liberal arts education, even in the early years when Booker T. Washington at Tuskegee Institute was promoting vocational education for blacks. A distinguished Fisk alumnus, W. E. B. DuBois, raised his voice on several occasions in support of Fisk's tradition of liberal education and in opposition to the vocational approach.

Fisk's position of relative financial and enrollment strength in the 1960s was lost through a combination of poor management and increased competition for black students and faculty from traditionally white colleges and universities. The low point occurred in November 1983, when utilities were shut off because of a back-debt in excess of $1 million. Henry Ponder arrived as president in July 1984, only to be advised by three bankruptcy judges to close the school. Through a combination of relentless cost cutting, strong community relations, and ingenious fund-raising, Ponder has managed to turn the college around financially. An unrestricted gift of $1.3 million from Bill Cosby in 1985 provided a critical vote of support, as did grants from the Lilly Endowment, the Kresge Foundation, AT&T, and the Ford Foundation. Annual support from the United Negro College Fund has been essential, as has federal support from Title III of the Higher Education Act, Aid for Developing Institutions. But the most interesting support by far is provided by the Department of Interior, which is financing the renovation of nine campus buildings, all on the National Register of Historic Buildings. Funds for Fisk are included as a line item in the Interior Department's budget. Support from the state's members of Congress helped to make this unusual appropriation possible.[9]

As noted in earlier chapters, historically black colleges have a radically different financing pattern from other private colleges; they rely much less heavily on tuition paid by families, and more heavily on federal student aid and support from Title III federal grants. Fisk is a remarkable example of determined leadership saving an institution that others were ready to write off. Fisk has paid off the debts accrued during the bleak years of the 1970s and early 1980s and is beginning

9. Such earmarking of appropriations for specific institutions, usually in connection with research facilities, has many critics in the education community.

to build endowment again. Enrollment is growing, and campus buildings will soon be in much better shape when renovations are finished. Having stared into the abyss, and survived, prospects for Fisk today are good.

Olivet

My site visit to Olivet in early April 1992 happened to coincide with a widely publicized racial brawl that occurred following a campus party. Over seventy students were involved, two were injured, and the incident captured national attention through radio, television, and newspaper accounts. It was especially damaging to the college that this unfortunate event happened when potential new students were deciding where to enroll. The incident and its aftermath cost Donald Morris, long-term president of Olivet, his job.

Olivet was founded in 1844 by individuals from Oberlin College, who sought to establish another center of learning on the Michigan frontier. The college has not yet been able to establish itself as one of the stronger colleges in Michigan, lagging behind Kalamazoo, Albion, Hope, and Alma. Enrollment in 1991 was 759, a number too low to provide much financial strength. Tables 6-1 and 6-2 indicate that the college did achieve a reasonable growth rate of net revenue (2.8 percent), while constraining spending to virtually no increase in real terms (0.4 percent annual growth). The pattern of outlays is disturbing, for instruction declined by 2.3 percent annually, while general administration (institutional support) increased by a substantial 7 percent a year. Olivet is the only college of the 12 visited in which per student spending on general administration ($3,046 in 1989) exceeded spending on instruction ($2,427 in 1989). Spending on operation and maintenance of physical plant also declined by a troubling 5.2 percent a year. By 1991, Olivet had lost all selectivity, admitting 610 of its 613 applicants, while experiencing only a 26 percent yield rate (table 5-4, chapter 5). To its credit, Olivet had achieved by 1991 an enrollment rate of African-American students of 9 percent, a higher percentage than most of the colleges in this study.

Olivet recently named a new president, a selection that is critical to its future. The college has very little maneuvering room left, financially or educationally. Among the colleges visited, prospects for Olivet are the least promising, and the new president and board of trustees will shoulder an enormous burden and responsibility in securing the institution's survival.

Problems That Lie Ahead

One purpose of the above vignettes is to give the reader a more direct understanding of the unique circumstances of each college, as well as the diverse situations found in this apparently homogeneous sector of higher education. The difficulty in generalizing about prospects for liberal arts colleges should be understandable after reading these stories. Nonetheless, there are some common issues that face these colleges in the 1990s that should be mentioned.

First, the pricing strategy described and analyzed in chapters 3 and 4 will be less beneficial in a time when annual tuition increases are lower than in the 1980s. For colleges in the data set, net tuition revenue increased by 3.2 percent a year in real terms between 1979 and 1989.[10] It will be difficult to sustain that pace at a time when tuition increases have declined to a rate between 5 percent and 6 percent. A simple example will suffice to make the point. Consider the case in which inflation is at 3 percent, tuition increases at 9 percent, and one-third of that increase is discounted as student aid; the result is a 3 percent gain in net tuition revenue, roughly the experience of the past decade. Assume now that inflation remains at 3 percent, tuition increases at 6 percent, and one-third of that increase is still discounted; the result is only a 1 percent gain in net tuition revenue, which is likely to approximate the experience of the past two years. Compounded annually over a decade, the difference between 1 percent and 3 percent growth is enormous. If colleges achieve only a 1 percent annual increase in net tuition revenue in the 1990s, they will be forced to hold spending tightly in check to maintain financial balance. Unless salaries are essentially frozen in real terms, a world of 1 percent gains in net tuition revenue will be marked by constant pressure to reduce educational spending. Attempts to cap (or reduce) unfunded student aid, however, in order to increase tuition income, will result in an end to need-blind admissions and diminished quality and diversity in the more selective colleges, and a drop in enrollments, and subsequent loss of revenue, in the less

10. See table 4-3, chapter 4.

selective colleges. This is a bind from which there is no obvious escape other than a return to the pricing policies of the 1980s, which poses additional problems and seems unlikely to happen.

It is also unlikely that the investment performance of the 1980s will be repeated in this decade, thereby reducing the fastest growing element in the revenue structure of most colleges during the past decade. (Gifts and endowment grew by 6.8 percent a year in real terms during the 1980s.)[11] In that case, the revenue source second only to tuition in importance for most colleges will support a smaller fraction of outlays in this decade than the last.

If the economy fails to rebound substantially, the growth of family incomes will remain depressed and may prompt more students to shift toward lower-priced public colleges and universities. The psychological impact of reduced job security on higher-income, professional families may also work its way into student decisions about college choice.

Finally, there seems little reason to expect substantial increases in spending on higher education from the federal government or from most state governments. The federal deficit is clearly structural as well as cyclical, and pressure to reduce the deficit seems likely to prevent Pell grants, for example, from growing significantly or becoming an entitlement program.[12] State budgets are strongly influenced by the economy and have been forced in recent years to absorb sharply higher spending for programs such as medicaid and prisons, reducing higher education to the role of residual claimant for shrinking discretionary funds. Thus, it would seem foolhardy to base financial planning for private colleges on an assumption that governmental spending will take up the slack created by reduced tuition and gift and endowment revenues.

Recommendations

This study was not intended to produce major policy recommendations or proposals for change; instead, the main purpose was to increase understanding of the forces operating on this small, but valuable, sector of American higher education. Certain points should be obvious and

11. See table 4-3, chapter 4.
12. Because funding for Pell grants is subject to annual appropriation, this program is not a true entitlement.

require little elaboration: current programs of federal and state aid, primarily in the form of grants and loans to students attending private colleges, are of enormous financial importance, and without them, many small colleges would long since have closed their doors. Gifts from private individuals, foundations, and corporations are especially valuable, providing the margin of excellence that enables a college to enhance the quality of its programs. Families who make a financial sacrifice to send children to private colleges are the true heroes of this story, for without them, nothing would remain. All these groups and individuals who believe strongly in the value of this type of higher education, and want to see it survive and flourish, clearly must continue to invest private and public resources in it. The importance of such gifts, grants, and tuition payments have been amply demonstrated in the quantitative analyses in this book.

Finally, advancing numerous, largely gratuitous, recommendations on college management and governance to those currently laboring in the vineyard would be presumptuous. One recommendation flowing directly from the study, however, must be made, for it would alter current practice. Throughout this book, student aid was netted out of the operating statements on revenue and expenditure sides to reveal more accurately the underlying financial relationships. Focusing on net tuition revenue is a far better way to study the effect of different pricing policies than to be misled by the accounting framework into believing that greater control exists over unfunded aid than is the case. Put bluntly, revenue that a college does not have and cannot get, cannot be controlled. Worrying about time trends in unfunded aid as a percentage of educational and general (E&G) expenditure, as if one could alter that trend without further damaging the finances of the college, is a wasted and pointless effort. The focus instead should be on trends in net tuition revenue, with unfunded aid measured separately as a percentage of gross tuition revenue, as discussed in chapter 3. There are enough legitimate things to worry about at these colleges without creating a crisis over the increase that occurred in the 1980s in unfunded aid as a fraction of E&G expenditure. The danger is that an attempt to control such aid by arbitrarily capping it at some percentage of outlays may cause enrollment to fall, leaving the college in worse financial shape. The modified accounting format used in chapters 3 and 4 can easily be adopted for use on campus and would

produce more economically sound analyses for management decisionmaking.

Conclusion

While it is not difficult to spin out a pessimistic scenario for many
private colleges in the 1990s, this review of past efforts reveals that
equally grim forecasts—ultimately inaccurate—have marked most of
their history. Economic analyses miss important intangible factors,
such as dedication, commitment, loyalty, sacrifice, and belief, which
typify and motivate many of those who support these schools. Private
colleges have many alumni, friends, and employees who believe in
them deeply, and an effective president can mobilize enormous support
when institutional survival is at stake. We have seen that the strongest
colleges are thriving, while most are surviving, and a few are endangered. (In particular, most colleges in the top two deciles of my analysis
appear to be thriving, those in deciles three through eight to be
surviving, while some in the bottom two deciles are endangered.) While
a keen eye on the economy and balance sheet is essential, it would be
a mistake to underestimate the intangible resources of these colleges
or to lose the faith that one can realistically have in their survival.

The 212 Colleges
in the Study

IN 1958 Earl J. McGrath and Charles H. Russell of Columbia Teachers College published a provocative monograph entitled, *Are Liberal Arts Colleges Becoming Professional Schools?*[1] This work had a significant impact on the thinking of educators at the time and is one of the few pieces of literature on higher education written in the 1950s that is still remembered today. McGrath and his associates were concerned about the status of the private liberal arts college and eventually became focused on the question, to what extent have professional programs entered the curricula of liberal arts colleges?

Their 1958 monograph, while listing by name the professional and preprofessional curricula offered in twenty-six liberal arts colleges in 1900 and 1957, provides no evidence on the extent of student enrollment in these professional fields, the number of majors undertaken in them, or even the number of colleges including them in the curriculum.

These omissions were corrected to some degree in a 1964 publication.[2] In a chapter entitled "The Quality and Cost of Liberal Arts College Programs: A Study of Twenty-Five Colleges," the authors present extensive data on the operating costs, staffing, and course distribution by department for this sample of colleges. In commenting on the distribution of courses offered by subject area, they write: "Since these are primarily liberal arts colleges, it is not surprising that they offer few professional courses. The few exceptions are primarily

1. Earl J. McGrath and Charles H. Russell, *Are Liberal Arts Colleges Becoming Professional Schools?* (Columbia University, Teachers College, 1958).

2. Earl J. McGrath, ed., *Cooperative Long-Range Planning in Liberal Arts Colleges* (Columbia University, Teachers College, 1964).

in education and business administration. The mean average indicates that the humanities subjects still constitute the largest area of instruction (36.3%), followed by the social sciences (28.4%), the natural sciences (22.6%), and finally, the professional subjects (12.7%)."[3] From these data it seems fair to suggest that McGrath and Russell's 1958 essay exaggerated considerably the extent to which liberal arts colleges of the 1950s had become professional schools. However, by the 1970s, the situation had clearly begun to change.

Curricular Change over Time

To learn more about the pattern of curricular change over time from liberal arts to professional studies, I analyzed degree data for 1972 and 1988. Figure A-1 shows the average percentage of professional bachelor's degrees awarded in those years by all 540 Liberal Arts I and Liberal Arts II colleges. Professional degrees include such fields as business, education, nursing, engineering, computer science, agriculture, and health sciences. For all colleges, professional degrees awarded rose from 33 percent in 1972 to 54 percent in 1988; for Liberal Arts I colleges, the figures are 11 percent and 24 percent respectively; and for Liberal Arts II colleges, 41 percent and 64 percent. By 1988, the answer to McGrath and Russell's question, are liberal arts colleges becoming professional schools, seems to be a resounding "yes" for a majority of colleges.

Chapter 1 notes that this shift toward professional degrees is found throughout higher education during the past two decades. In 1986 only one in four bachelor's degrees was awarded in the liberal arts. This shift is also mirrored in changing student attitudes toward higher education as figure A-2 shows.

The shift from liberal arts fields to professional education was a dominant strategy followed by hundreds of private colleges since 1972 to ensure their survival. The change has been so pronounced that it seems mistaken to call such schools liberal arts colleges any more. According to a liberal definition that calls any school awarding less than 60 percent of its degrees in professional fields a liberal arts college, there are only about 200 of them left in this country. (Were a more

3. McGrath, *Cooperative Long-Range Planning*, p. 14.

Figure A-1. *Professional Degrees Awarded by Liberal Arts Colleges, 1972, 1988*

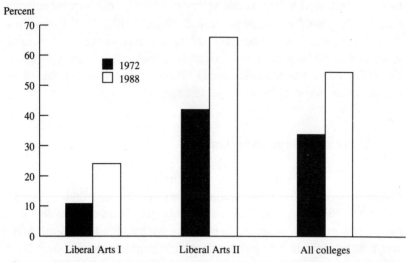

Percent

■ 1972
□ 1988

Liberal Arts I   Liberal Arts II   All colleges

Source: Author's calculations based on data from the National Center for Higher Education Systems, Boulder, Colorado.

rigorous definition applied, such as including only those colleges that awarded less than 25 percent of its degrees in professional fields, there would be fewer than 90 liberal arts colleges.) The 60 percent definition is used to identify the colleges included in this book. We should, however, consider briefly criticisms that have been leveled at a definition based primarily on major fields of study.

Alternative Definitions

Several rejoinders were published in the *College Board Review* and in the *American Association of Higher Education Bulletin* to my earlier article, "Are We Losing Our Liberal Arts Colleges?"[4] Critics of my definition most often pointed out that the major field typically occupies

4. The article appeared in the *College Board Review*, no. 156 (Summer 1990), pp. 17–21, and was reprinted in the October 1990 issue of the *AAHE Bulletin*. Rejoinders were published in the Fall 1990 and Winter 1990–91 issues of *College Board Review* and in the December 1990 issue of the *AAHE Bulletin*.

Figure A-2. *Trends in the Life Goals of Freshmen*

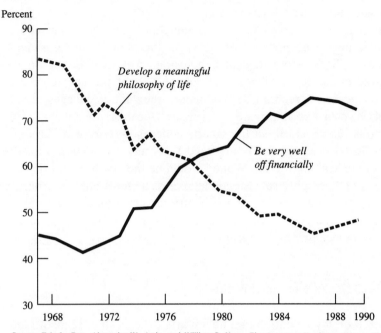

Source: Eric L. Dey, Alexander W. Astin, and William S. Korn, *The American Freshman: Twenty-Five Year Trends, 1966–1990* (University of California, Los Angeles, Higher Education Research Institute of the Graduate School of Education, 1991).

no more than one-third of a student's course work, and that the underlying general education courses provide a liberal education regardless of major:

> But since when have we based the definition of a liberal arts education solely on the major? At most institutions the major constitutes only a fourth to a third of a student's program, with the greater part of baccalaureate studies in general education and electives. The fact that many students today are in professional or preprofessional courses does not necessarily mean that they accomplish less study in the liberal arts.[5]

Others argued that the distinction between liberal and professional fields was largely arbitrary and subject to change; one era's professional education is another's liberal education. Still others argued that the

5. Allen P. Splete and Russell Y. Garth, "Extinction, or Evolution?" *AAHE Bulletin*, vol. 43 (December 1990), p. 12.

true challenge facing liberal arts colleges was to integrate liberal and professional studies.[6]

These are reasonable comments, highlighting some of the key educational issues being debated on many of the nation's undergraduate campuses. Taken to a logical conclusion, they cast doubt on the meaning of the term "liberal arts college," for if the subject matter studied bears no relation to that name, then these colleges should simply be called small private colleges, or baccalaureate colleges. This is a book, however, about liberal arts colleges, a term to which I can attach little meaning if it is divorced from any connection with the type of curriculum offered. While I would be the first to admit that the choice of 60 percent professional degrees as a cutoff point is arbitrary (and a case could be made for a stricter criterion), I believe the definition employed is both defensible and true to the historical and traditional meaning of the term.

The 212 Colleges in this Study

Based on my definition of a liberal arts college, the 212 institutions included in this study are listed alphabetically in table A-1. Besides the information provided for each college in table A-1, the following statistics help to describe the colleges that make up this group.

Enrollment

The average (mean) enrollment in 1990–91 for these 212 colleges was 1,224, while the median was 1,116. The largest college was St. Olaf, with 3,097 students, while the smallest was Goddard, with 260.[7] One college enrolled more than 3,000 students—St. Olaf—while 26 enrolled between 2,000 and 3,000, and 83 enrolled fewer than 1,000. Seventy percent (148) of the colleges enroll less than 10 percent part-time students, while eight—Caldwell, Immaculata, Lourdes, Mary-

6. James A. Appleton and Frank F. Wong in the *College Board Review*, no. 157 (Fall 1990), p. 26; John Jacobson, "Redefining Our Institution," p. 26; and S. Fredrick Starr, "Liberal Arts Are Flourising," *College Board Review*, no. 158 (Winter 1990–91), p. 28.

7. Both Goddard and Marlboro colleges enrolled fewer than 300 students in 1990–91, but were larger than 300 students in 1985–86 when the selections were made.

mount Manhattan, Mundelein, Neumann, Rockford, and Wilson—enroll more than 50 percent part-time students.

Location

The colleges are located in thirty-nine states and the District of Columbia. The largest number of colleges, 74, are in the northeastern region, while the north central region has 62, southern and south central region 60, and the western region only 16. The ten states with the largest number of colleges are Pennsylvania, 22; New York, 19; Illinois, 16; Massachusetts, 14; Ohio, 11; California, 10; Virginia, 10; Michigan, 8; North Carolina, 8; and Tennessee, 8.

Religious Affiliation

Most of the colleges, 124, report that they are affiliated with an organized religion. The largest number, 27, are connected with the Presbyterian church, while 26 are affiliated with the Methodist church (including United Methodist), 19 with the Roman Catholic church, 10 with the Lutheran church, and smaller numbers with other Protestant religions, including Baptist, Disciples of Christ, Episcopalian, Evangelical Lutheran, Quaker, and United Church of Christ. Of the remaining 88 nonaffiliated colleges, most began under religious auspices but subsequently dropped the explicit connection.

Gender and Race

Twenty-five of the institutions are women's colleges, while only three (Hampden-Sydney, Morehouse, and Wabash) are men's colleges. The women's colleges are (in alphabetical order): Agnes Scott, Barnard, Bennett, Chatham, Chestnut Hill, Emmanuel, Hollins, Judson (Alabama), Mary Baldwin, Mills, Mount Holyoke, Pine Manor, Randolph-Macon Woman's, Regis, Rosemont, Salem, Scripps, Smith, Spelman, St. Mary-of-the-Woods, Sweet Briar, Trinity (D.C.), Wellesley, Wells, and Wesleyan (Georgia). (Women also make up 90 percent or more of the enrollment at four other colleges—Immaculata, Marymount Manhattan, Mundelein, and Seton Hill—but these schools are not included in our analyses of women's colleges.) Twelve historically black colleges are in the data set—Barber-Scotia, Claflin, Fisk,

Table A-1. 212 Colleges, 1990–91

Institution	Founded	Enroll-ment	Percent part-time	Women students	Percent women	Black students	Percent black	Affiliation
Adrian College	1859	1,187	8	677	57	47	4	Methodist
Agnes Scott College	1889	593	13	593	100	59	10	Presbyterian
Albertus Magnus College	1925	505	7	354	70	30	6	Roman Catholic
Albion College	1835	1,643	0	805	49	33	2	Methodist
Albright College	1856	1,253	6	652	52	50	4	Methodist
Allegheny College	1815	1,798	2	935	52	54	3	Methodist
Alma College	1886	1,227	2	663	54	12	1	Presbyterian
Amherst College	1821	1,580	0	727	46	111	7	...
Augustana College	1860	2,253	1	1,239	55	68	3	Presbyterian
Austin College	1849	1,230	2	615	50	25	2	Presbyterian
Barat College	1858	685	41	514	75	55	8	Roman Catholic
Barber-Scotia College	1867	n.a.	n.a.	n.a.	n.a.	n.a.	100	Presbyterian
Bard College	1860	1,068	8	545	51	107	10	...
Barnard College	1889	2,200	0	2,200	100	88	4	...
Bates College	1855	1,500	1	750	50	30	2	...
Beloit College	1846	1,053	1	579	55	32	3	...
Benedictine College	1859	800	8	384	48	32	4	Roman Catholic
Bennett College	1873	572	17	572	100	n.a.	n.a.	Methodist
Bennington College	1932	580	1	348	60	17	3	...
Bethany College	1840	859	5	430	50	43	5	Disciples of Christ
Bethel College, Kansas	1887	570	15	319	56	23	4	Mennonite
Bethel College, Tenn.	1842	525	31	299	57	42	8	Presbyterian
Birmingham-Southern College	1856	1,800	3	1,026	57	162	9	Methodist
Blackburn College	1837	428	4	210	49	43	10	Presbyterian
Bowdoin College	1794	1,350	1	581	43	54	4	...
Bradford College	1803	475	15	247	52	24	5	...
Bridgewater College	1880	1,007	5	564	56	20	2	Church of the Brethren

College	Year							Affiliation
Bryan College	1930	502	17	251	50	10	2	...
Caldwell College	1939	1,186	53	771	65	95	8	Roman Catholic
California Baptist College	1950	637	16	331	52	45	7	Southern Baptist
Carleton College	1866	1,707	0	819	48	51	3	...
Carroll College, Wisconsin	1846	1,495	0	897	60	45	3	Presbyterian
Centenary College of Louisiana	1825	795	6	405	51	8	1	Methodist
Centre College of Kentucky	1819	880	1	440	50	18	2	Presbyterian
Chatham College	1869	643	33	643	100	64	10	...
Chestnut Hill College	1924	850	37	850	100	68	8	Roman Catholic
Christ College Irvine	1972	516	6	299	58	15	3	Lutheran
Christian Heritage	1970	327	5	160	49	7	2	Baptist
Claflin College	1869	887	3	532	60	878	99	Methodist
Claremont McKenna College	1946	847	0	322	38	42	5	...
Coe College	1851	1,250	20	613	49	38	3	Presbyterian
Coker College	1908	778	32	475	61	218	28	...
Colby College	1813	1,741	2	871	50	35	2	...
Colgate University	1819	2,698	1	1,241	46	135	5	...
College of Mt. St. Vincent	1847	1,022	38	828	81	123	12	Roman Catholic
College of the Holy Cross	1843	2,738	0	1,369	50	110	4	Roman Catholic
College of Wooster	1866	1,804	0	920	51	108	6	Presbyterian
Colorado College	1874	1,933	0	1,005	52	39	2	...
Concordia College, Mich.	1963	593	1	332	56	6	1	Lutheran
Concordia College, N.Y.	1881	403	6	238	59	44	11	Lutheran
Connecticut College	1911	1,904	12	1,066	56	76	4	...
Cornell College	1853	1,140	1	604	53	23	2	Methodist
Dana College	1884	507	13	279	55	35	7	Evangelical Lutheran
Davidson College	1837	1,508	0	603	40	60	4	Presbyterian
Denison University	1831	2,015	1	1,048	52	101	5	...
Depauw University	1837	2,347	1	1,314	56	141	6	Methodist
Dickinson College	1773	2,003	0	1,142	57	20	1	...
Earlham College	1847	1,148	1	654	57	92	8	Quaker

Table A-1 (continued)

Institution	Founded	Enroll-ment	Percent part-time	Women students	Percent women	Black students	Percent black	Affiliation
Eckerd College	1958	1,370	2	712	52	41	3	Presbyterian
Emmanuel College	1919	902	28	902	100	108	12	Roman Catholic
Emory and Henry College	1836	844	5	405	48	17	2	Methodist
Fisk University	1866	888	0	577	65	870	98	United Church of Christ
Flagler College	1968	1,188	n.a.	677	57	12	1	. . .
Franklin and Marshall	1787	1,807	3	813	45	54	3	. . .
Franklin College of Indiana	1834	880	8	466	53	35	4	American Baptist
Furman University	1826	2,462	6	1,305	53	74	3	Baptist
Gettysburg College	1832	1,950	1	975	50	59	3	Evangelical Lutheran
Goddard College	1938	260	0	138	53	21	8	. . .
Gordon College	1889	1,150	4	679	59	23	2	Interdenominational
Goshen College	1894	1,042	10	573	55	52	5	Mennonite
Goucher College	1885	888	13	684	77	36	4	. . .
Greensboro College	1838	1,116	24	703	63	112	10	Methodist
Greenville College	1892	849	7	408	48	42	5	Free Methodist
Grinnell College	1846	1,251	0	600	48	50	4	. . .
Guilford College	1837	1,368	3	698	51	82	6	Quaker
Gustavus Adolphus College	1862	2,320	2	1,253	54	46	2	Evangelical Lutheran
Hamilton College	1812	1,668	1	784	47	67	4	. . .
Hampden-Sydney College	1776	956	0	0	0	19	2	Presbyterian
Hampshire College	1965	1,263	0	733	58	38	3	. . .
Hanover College	1827	1,064	2	553	52	11	1	Presbyterian
Hartwick College	1797	1,498	2	884	59	15	1	. . .
Haverford College	1833	1,147	0	505	44	57	5	. . .
Hawaii Loa College	1963	625[a]	18	400	64	25	4	Interdenominational
Heidelberg College	1850	1,340	9	697	52	54	4	United Church of Christ
Hendrix College	1876	1,006	n.a.	543	54	60	6	Methodist

College	Year							Denomination
Hillsdale College	1844	5	1,110	577	52	11	1	....
Hiram College	1850	n.a.	900	750	56	80	6	Disciples of Christ
Hobart-William Smith Colleges	1822	1	1,838	809	44	110	6	Episcopal
Hollins College	1842	7	922	922	100	18	2	....
Hope College	1862	11	2,813	1,575	56	28	1	Reformed Church
Houghton College	1883	4	1,170	714	61	23	2	Wesleyan
Huntingdon College	1854	22	791	475	60	40	5	Methodist
Illinois College	1829	2	888	426	48	18	2	Interdenominational
Immaculata College	1920	50	2,050	1,948	95	144	7	Roman Catholic
Jamestown College	1883	6	899	467	52	9	1	Presbyterian
Judson College, Alabama	1838	8	420	420	100	21	5	Baptist
Judson College, Illinois	1963	0	515	278	54	n.a.	n.a.	Baptist
Juniata College	1876	4	1,146	619	54	11	1	....
Kalamazoo College	1833	0	1,265	696	55	38	3	....
Kenyon College	1824	0	1,506	768	51	60	4	....
King College	1867	6	535	278	52	5	1	Presbyterian (U.S.A.)
Knox College	1837	2	1,029	515	50	51	5	....
Lafayette College	1826	12	1,960	882	45	78	4	Presbyterian (U.S.A.)
Lake Forest College	1857	1	1,095	558	51	88	8	....
Lawrence University	1847	3	1,235	605	49	37	3	....
Lebanon Valley College	1866	25	830	382	46	8	1	Methodist
LeMoyne-Owen College	1870	11	1,066	746	70	1055	99	United Church of Christ
Long Is. U., Southampton Campus	1963	10	1,164	687	59	105	9	....
Lourdes College	1958	75	1,049	881	84	42	4	Roman Catholic
Luther College	1861	4	2,265	1,336	59	45	2	Evangelical Lutheran
Lycoming College	1812	3	1,271	610	48	13	1	Methodist
Macalester College	1874	6	1,853	1,001	54	74	4	Presbyterian
MacMurray College	1846	9	611	336	55	37	6	Methodist
Manhattanville College	1841	19	1,354	880	65	95	7	....
Marlboro College	1947	4	291	154	53	6	2	....
Mary Baldwin College	1842	1	677	677	100	14	2	Presbyterian (U.S.A.)

Table A-1 (*continued*)

Institution	Founded	Enroll-ment	Percent part-time	Women students	Percent women	Black students	Percent black	Affiliation
Marymount Manhattan College	1936	1,300	50	1,170	90	221	17	. . .
Maryville College	1819	735	13	390	53	37	5	Presbyterian
Middlebury College	1800	1,950	1	975	50	78	4	. . .
Miles College	1905	616	24	326	53	610	99	Chrst. Method. Epis.
Mills College	1852	744	3	744	100	60	8	. . .
Millsaps College	1890	1,289	12	606	47	52	4	Methodist
Monmouth College, Illinois	1853	676	5	338	50	68	10	Presbyterian
Morehouse College	1867	2,720	8	0	0	2,638	97	. . .
Morris College	1908	760	2	502	66	760	100	Baptist
Mount Holyoke College	1837	1,879	1	1,879	100	75	4	. . .
Mount Ida College	1899	1,800	5	1,170	65	180	10	. . .
Muhlenberg College	1848	1,638	4	983	60	33	2	Lutheran
Mundelein College	1929	917	53	862	94	193	21	Roman Catholic
Muskingum College	1837	1,092	4	513	47	22	2	Presbyterian (U.S.A.)
Nebraska Wesleyan University	1887	1,684	18	960	57	17	1	Methodist
Neumann College	1965	1,206	58	917	76	60	5	Roman Catholic
North Park College	1891	900	9	486	54	45	5	Evangelical Covenant
Northland College	1892	758	6	356	47	8	1	United Church of Christ
Oberlin College	1833	2,805	2	1,431	51	224	8	. . .
Occidental College	1887	1,664	1	865	52	67	4	. . .
Oglethorpe University	1835	1,036	33	622	60	41	4	. . .
Ohio Wesleyan University	1842	2,040	3	1,020	50	102	5	Methodist
Olivet College	1844	759	10	334	44	68	9	Congregational
Palm Beach Atlantic College	1968	1,375	20	729	53	138	10	Southern Baptist
Piedmont College	1897	495	16	267	54	25	5	Congregational
Pine Manor College	1911	590	5	590	100	30	5	. . .
Pitzer College	1963	750	5	390	52	45	6	. . .

College								
Pomona College	1887	1,375	0	701	51	55	4	· · ·
Presbyterian College	1880	1,136	5	534	47	57	5	Presbyterian
Principia College	1910	622	3	373	60	6	1	Christian Science
Randolph-Macon College	1830	1,141	2	616	54	34	3	Methodist
Randolph-Macon Woman's	1891	700	8	700	100	14	2	Methodist
Reed College	1909	1,275	4	548	43	26	2	· · ·
Regis College, Mass.	1927	1,163	33	1,163	100	35	3	Roman Catholic
Rhodes College	1848	1,407	5	760	54	56	4	Presbyterian
Ripon College	1851	854	3	418	49	9	1	· · ·
Roanoke College	1842	1,668	12	967	58	17	1	Evangelical Lutheran
Roberts Wesleyan College	1866	969	11	581	60	58	6	Free Methodist
Rockford College	1847	1,123	64	775	69	34	3	· · ·
Rosemont College	1921	702	20	702	100	21	3	Roman Catholic
Salem College	1772	694	16	694	100	21	3	Moravian
Sarah Lawrence College	1926	1,050	10	788	75	95	9	· · ·
Scripps College	1926	629	1	629	100	19	3	· · ·
Seton Hill College	1883	1,037	30	933	90	31	3	Roman Catholic
Shorter College	1873	841	14	555	66	42	5	Baptist
Skidmore College	1903	2,139	n.a.	1,198	56	64	3	· · ·
Smith College	1871	2,662	5	2,662	100	106	4	· · ·
Southwestern University	1840	1,239	2	681	55	37	3	Methodist
Spelman College	1881	1,708	1	1,708	100	1,691	99	· · ·
Spring Hill College	1830	1,054	3	538	51	42	4	Roman Catholic
St. Andrews Presbyterian College	1958	716	8	365	51	43	6	Presbyterian
St. Anselm College	1889	1,840	6	975	53	18	1	Roman Catholic
St. John's College, Annapolis	1696	392	1	172	44	12	3	· · ·
St. John's College, Santa Fe	1964	400	2	180	45	4	1	· · ·
St. John's University	1857	1,971	3	20	1	20	1	Roman Catholic
St. Lawrence University	1856	2,111	7	1,077	51	63	3	· · ·
St. Mary-of-the-Woods College	1840	1,018	70	1,018	100	51	5	Roman Catholic
St. Olaf College	1874	3,097	3	1,641	53	31	1	Lutheran

Table A-1 (continued)

Institution	Founded	Enrollment	Percent part-time	Women students	Percent women	Black students	Percent black	Affiliation
Swarthmore College	1864	1,317	0	672	51	92	7	...
Sweet Briar College	1901	539	6	539	100	22	4	...
Talladega College	1867	615	7	412	67	597	97	...
Thiel College	1866	931	16	475	51	47	5	Evangelical Lutheran
Thomas More College	1921	1,297	39	765	59	52	4	Roman Catholic
Tougaloo College	1869	948	3	616	65	939	99	Interdenominational
Transylvania University	1780	1,091	10	546	50	22	2	Disciples of Christ
Trinity College, Conn.	1823	1,945	11	953	49	136	7	...
Trinity College, D.C.	1897	1,000	n.a.	1,000	100	80	8	Roman Catholic
Trinity College, Illinois	1897	914	6	430	47	73	8	Evangelical Free Church
Union College, New York	1795	2,000	0	880	44	60	3	...
University of the South	1857	1,096	2	504	46	11	1	Episcopal
Ursinus College	1869	1,073	2	569	53	32	3	United Church of Christ
Vassar College	1861	2,308	7	1,292	56	185	8	...
Vermont College (Norwich Univ.)	1819	2,047	10	655	32	41	2	...
Virginia Wesleyan College	1961	1,390	19	890	64	70	5	Methodist
Voorhees College	1897	575	3	431	75	569	99	Episcopal
Wabash College	1832	854	1	0	0	34	4	...
Warner Pacific College	1937	496	20	253	51	15	3	Church of God
Warren Wilson College	1894	502	1	306	61	15	3	Presbyterian (U.S.A.)
Wartburg College	1852	1,440	6	749	52	29	2	Lutheran
Washington College	1782	923	6	508	55	18	2	...
Washington and Jefferson College	1781	1,205	3	494	41	48	4	...
Wellesley College	1870	2,279	7	2,279	100	160	7	...

Wells College	1868	400	4	400	100	20	5	. . .
Wesleyan College	1836	540	18	540	100	54	10	Methodist
Wesleyan University	1831	2,709	0	1,355	50	244	9	. . .
Western Maryland College	1867	1,315	8	684	52	39	3	. . .
Westminster College	1851	786	7	267	34	16	2	Presbyterian
Westmont College	1940	1,264	1	746	59	13	1	. . .
Wheaton College, Ill.	1860	2,235	1	1,185	53	22	1	. . .
Wheaton College, Mass.	1834	1,264	3	973	77	38	3	. . .
Whitman College	1859	1,267	1	659	52	13	1	. . .
Wilberforce University	1856	805	0	547	68	773	96	African Methodist Episcopal
Williams College	1793	2,069	1	931	45	166	8	. . .
Wilson College	1869	853	70	682	80	9	1	Presbyterian
Wittenberg University	1845	2,350	2	1,269	54	165	7	Evangelical Lutheran
Wofford College	1854	1,076	3	420	39	86	8	Methodist

Source: *Peterson's Guide to Four-Year Colleges 1992*, 22d ed. (Princeton, N.J.: Peterson's Guides, Inc., 1991); and *Barron's Profiles of American Colleges*, 18th ed. (Woodbury, N.Y.: Barron's Educational Series, 1991).
n.a. Not available.
a. 43 percent white.

Le Moyne-Owen, Miles, Morehouse, Morris, Spelman, Talladega, Tougaloo, Voorhees, and Wilberforce—with black students accounting for 96 percent or more of their enrollments.

Women account for 57.8 percent of the total enrollment in these 212 colleges, while blacks make up 8.6 percent of the total. Black students are concentrated in the historically black institutions, however, with small numbers enrolled in most of the colleges in the data set. When black enrollments are rank-ordered, the median college has only 4 percent black students. Among the 212 colleges, 153 have less than 6 percent black students, 84 have less than 3 percent, and 28 have 1 percent or less enrolled. Clearly private liberal arts colleges are not playing a significant role in educating large numbers of African-American students, nor does that fact seem likely to change in the near future.

Data Sources

Data for this study came from three sources—the National Center for Education Statistics (NCES), the College Board, and site visits to the twelve colleges. NCES financial and enrollment data were provided by two other research organizations, the National Center for Higher Education Management Systems (NCHEMS) in Boulder, Colorado, and the Williams Project on the Economics of Higher Education at Williams College, Massachusetts. The analyses of enrollment, tuition, and financial aid in chapter 3 draw on financial and enrollment data provided by NCHEMS,[8] as well as data on applications, admissions, and enrollments provided by the College Board. The financial analyses in chapter 4 primarily draw on the Williams College data file, which covers two academic years—1978–79 (referred to as 1979), and 1988–89 (referred to as 1989). The data are constructed as a panel, so that only those colleges with data for both years are included. Of the 212 colleges in this study, 181 are included in the Williams College data set.

The College Board office in New York provided data on tuition charges and on the number of applications, acceptances, and enrollments for the colleges in this study for selected years between 1976–

8. These data are drawn from the Higher Education General Information Survey (HEGIS) and Integrated Postsecondary Education Data System (IPEDS), collected by the National Center for Education Statistics, Washington.

77 and 1990–91. (The Higher Education General Information Survey [HEGIS] and the Integrated Postsecondary Education Data System [IPEDS] data record total tuition revenues, but not the actual tuition price.) The College Board data are used both in the rankings presented later in this chapter and in the enrollment analyses of chapter 3.

Finally, site visits at 12 colleges provided additional quantitative data of various types, depending on the significance of the item for the particular college. My purpose in visiting the colleges was not to collect historical data but rather to focus on plans for the future; however, I inevitably collected local data, and these are used when relevant in the discussions of the site visit colleges in Chapters 5 and 6.

Rankings by Financial and Enrollment Strength

The analyses in chapters 3 and 4 examine the economic impact of the last decade on subsets of liberal arts colleges, including women's colleges, historically black colleges, and religiously affiliated colleges. To achieve a more complete understanding of this sector, however, it seemed equally important to have some way of grouping the colleges by relative financial and enrollment strength. Such measures do not come ready made and thus had to be constructed. I selected three measures as capturing these elements—endowment for each full-time equivalent (FTE) student, net tuition revenue for each FTE student, and the ratio of acceptances to applications for the entering class.

The endowment measure captures a significant wealth variable, which varies dramatically among these colleges. Endowment/FTE tells us something about the nontuition revenues that are available to strengthen the quality of education provided, as well as providing a buffer against financial hard times.[9] Net tuition/FTE is a measure of the financial strength and drawing power of a college. It is constructed by subtracting from gross tuition revenues the amount of nonendowed student financial aid (effectively tuition discounts) to determine the actual net tuition revenue received by the college.[10] Although colleges

9. This latter function is more properly filled by that part of endowment known as quasi endowment, which may be spent at the discretion of trustees.

10. Fund accounting for colleges on the revenue side assumes that all students pay full tuition, with institutional sources of financial aid treated as an expense. Nonendowed financial aid provided by the college must be netted off against gross tuition to determine net tuition revenue.

Table A-2. *College Rankings*[a]

Group and institution	Net tuition	Rank	Endowment	Rank	Percent of applicants accepted	Rank	Composite rank
1 Middlebury College	14,276	1	105,961	11	28	5	17
1 Amherst College	11,022	12	167,754	5	19	1	18
1 Bowdoin College	11,661	8	101,661	12	22	2	22
1 Williams College	10,755	23	149,454	7	24	3	33
1 Claremont McKenna College	11,764	7	108,339	10	37	16	33
1 Pomona College	11,015	13	190,748	4	39	19	36
1 Swarthmore College	10,752	24	225,082	3	34	10	37
1 Wesleyan University	10,954	14	88,945	17	32	9	40
1 Wellesley College	12,338	2	160,394	6	48	32	40
1 Carleton College	11,039	11	83,447	21	41	22	54
1 Hamilton College	11,803	6	69,948	26	42	23	55
1 Colby College	11,932	5	43,177	42	35	13	60
1 Trinity College, Conn.	12,218	3	68,458	30	44	29	62
1 Lafayette College	10,207	32	94,551	15	37	17	64
1 Haverford College	10,632	26	72,626	25	35	15	66
1 Bates College	11,954	4	37,412	53	34	11	68
1 Colgate University	10,782	21	45,419	41	30	7	69
1 Vassar College	9,809	38	98,177	13	39	18	69
1 Smith College	10,898	17	111,177	9	55	46	72
2 Colorado College	9,385	43	62,446	32	35	14	89
2 Oberlin College	10,953	15	78,976	23	57	55	93
2 Davidson College	8,873	54	57,150	37	30	6	97
2 Mount Holyoke College	10,412	27	85,926	20	57	53	100
2 Franklin and Marshall	10,117	34	42,914	44	43	26	104
2 Union College	10,075	35	38,736	50	39	20	105
2 University of the South	10,650	25	81,312	22	61	63	110

2	Scripps College	10,757	22	94,155	16	67	78	116
2	College of the Holy Cross	9,627	41	30,279	69	34	12	122
2	St. Lawrence University	11,048	10	40,677	47	63	68	125
2	Reed College	8,922	53	59,005	34	52	42	129
2	Grinnell College	7,838	70	226,974	2	58	57	129
2	Dickinson College	10,376	28	22,010	85	40	21	134
2	Denison University	9,318	46	35,382	55	49	34	135
2	Occidental College	7,621	72	86,710	19	57	54	145
2	Macalester College	9,249	49	33,798	60	51	39	148
2	Lawrence University	8,729	56	58,897	35	59	60	151
2	Barnard College	10,269	30	21,021	89	49	35	154
2	Hobart-William Smith Colleges	10,869	18	16,828	106	48	33	157
3	Kenyon College	10,148	33	21,526	87	50	37	157
3	Connecticut College	10,007	37	19,642	95	44	28	160
3	Lake Forest College	9,360	44	26,374	75	51	41	160
3	Gettysburg College	10,287	29	17,786	102	47	30	161
3	Pitzer College	10,833	19	18,639	99	56	47	165
3	Skidmore College	10,821	20	12,884	122	43	25	167
3	Hampden-Sydney College	8,373	61	32,425	62	57	50	173
3	College of Wooster	8,178	63	38,859	49	61	64	176
3	Sweet Briar College	9,749	39	87,431	18	81	129	186
3	Wheaton College, Ill.	6,968	86	34,388	58	56	48	192
3	Sarah Lawrence College	10,918	16	11,681	126	57	52	194
3	Furman University	7,019	84	27,391	73	51	40	197
3	Depauw University	9,340	45	31,873	63	71	89	197
3	Randolph-Macon Woman's	8,588	57	62,347	33	77	110	200
3	Goucher College	8,995	52	68,885	29	79	119	200
3	Hartwick College	8,405	60	28,489	72	64	73	205
3	Hollins College	8,118	65	40,903	46	73	95	206
3	Chatham College	5,800	134	69,731	27	57	51	212
3	Hampshire College	9,510	42	8,084	141	47	31	214

Table A-2 (continued)

Group and institution	Net tuition	Rank	Endowment	Rank	Percent of applicants accepted	Rank	Composite rank
4 Wheaton College, Mass.	9,720	40	37,908	52	80	123	215
4 Centre College of Kentucky	6,571	104	53,120	39	65	76	219
4 Muhlenberg College	8,870	55	16,357	110	58	56	221
4 St. John's College, Annapolis	9,299	47	50,352	40	82	134	221
4 Whitman College	7,887	68	74,174	24	81	131	223
4 Rhodes College	6,180	121	57,738	36	64	72	229
4 St. Olaf College	7,962	66	10,684	129	51	38	233
4 Ohio Wesleyan University	7,258	80	23,014	84	63	70	234
4 Bennington College	11,175	9	5,987	161	61	65	235
4 Washington College	8,425	59	20,422	92	68	84	235
4 Spelman College	4,557	159	29,765	70	32	8	237
4 Mills College	8,157	64	69,330	28	83	145	237
4 Roanoke College	6,882	89	17,165	103	56	49	241
4 Randolph-Macon College	6,997	85	20,840	90	62	66	241
4 Ursinus College	5,858	133	23,420	82	43	27	242
4 Eckerd College	9,079	50	7,248	151	54	43	244
4 Agnes Scott College	6,489	108	239,165	1	82	135	244
4 Washington and Jefferson College	8,465	58	28,742	71	79	118	247
4 Allegheny College	8,303	62	24,084	80	77	109	251
5 Bard College	9,252	48	5,779	163	55	45	256
5 Wittenberg University	7,854	69	17,039	104	71	91	264
5 Southwestern University	4,840	154	95,475	14	73	96	264
5 Knox College	7,337	79	25,990	76	77	112	267
5 Albright College	7,491	76	9,757	134	59	59	269
5 Austin College	6,752	93	54,830	38	82	138	269
5 Beloit College	7,346	77	27,068	74	81	124	275

5	Kalamazoo College	7,770	71	30,889	68	82	136	275
5	Manhattanville College	7,896	67	16,768	107	74	102	276
5	Presbyterian College	6,145	122	24,250	79	67	80	281
5	St. John's College, Santa Fe	9,056	51	21,838	86	83	144	281
5	Monmouth College	7,252	81	25,779	77	81	126	284
5	Western Maryland College	7,563	73	7,918	144	64	71	288
5	Wells College	6,788	92	68,408	31	86	166	289
5	Bradford College	6,719	96	16,907	105	74	100	301
5	Cornell College	6,660	100	19,877	94	77	108	302
5	Wabash College	5,017	153	146,732	8	83	142	303
5	Guilford College	6,340	114	13,735	115	65	75	304
5	Coe College	5,549	141	34,419	57	78	113	311
6	Juniata College	7,535	75	21,036	88	84	148	311
6	Lycoming College	6,805	90	16,352	111	77	111	312
6	Hendrix College	4,394	165	43,135	43	76	107	315
6	Pine Manor College	10,265	31	11,217	128	85	157	316
6	Franklin College Indiana	4,761	157	32,881	61	74	99	317
6	Albion College	7,071	82	31,705	64	88	171	317
6	Gustavus Adolphus College	7,038	83	8,927	138	73	97	318
6	Rosemont College	6,514	106	11,482	127	70	88	321
6	Marymount Manhattan	10,064	36	2,293	179	76	106	321
6	Bethany College	6,728	94	31,080	67	85	161	322
6	Regis College	6,723	95	31,632	66	86	163	324
6	Hiram College	6,199	120	19,642	96	79	117	333
6	Salem College	5,679	137	24,602	78	79	120	335
6	Flagler College	3,665	177	9,156	137	43	24	338
6	Concordia College, Mich.	5,926	128	3,627	175	50	36	339
6	Bridgewater College	5,020	152	16,761	108	67	79	339
6	Coker College	4,412	164	23,277	83	72	93	340
6	Palm Beach Atlantic College	4,350	167	18,007	100	65	74	341
6	Transylvania University	6,206	119	41,853	45	90	177	341

Table A-2 (continued)

Group and institution	Net tuition	Rank	Endowment	Rank	Percent of applicants accepted	Rank	Composite rank
7 Wofford College	5,663	139	12,666	123	67	81	343
7 Heidelberg College	6,435	110	8,779	140	73	94	344
7 Talladega College	2,827	184	13,133	118	54	44	346
7 Wilson College	5,196	147	16,483	109	71	92	348
7 Alma College	6,271	116	35,599	54	90	178	348
7 St. Anselm College	6,527	105	2,882	178	63	69	352
7 Millsaps College	6,883	88	19,515	97	86	168	353
7 Tougaloo College	3,070	182	4,302	169	26	4	355
7 Morehouse College	4,492	161	14,968	113	68	82	356
7 Lebanon Valley College	6,046	125	9,907	133	74	98	356
7 Muskingum College	6,420	111	14,300	114	82	137	362
7 Ripon College	6,393	112	20,614	91	85	159	362
7 North Park College	6,587	103	6,755	158	75	103	364
7 Emory and Henry College	5,657	140	20,217	93	81	132	365
7 Illinois College	4,376	166	33,911	59	83	140	365
7 St. John's University	6,796	91	13,601	116	85	158	365
7 Birmingham Southern	5,724	135	24,007	81	84	153	369
7 Wilberforce University	4,777	156	7,161	153	61	62	371
7 Augustana College	6,689	98	7,977	143	81	130	371
8 Barat College	6,666	99	881	190	70	86	375
8 Centenary of Louisiana	4,512	160	38,895	48	86	167	375
8 Mundelein College	7,340	78	1,960	184	78	114	376
8 Westmont College	6,716	97	5,130	165	78	115	377
8 Hope College	6,649	101	9,262	135	83	141	377
8 Westminster College	4,475	162	31,683	65	85	155	382
8 Concordia College, N.Y.	5,895	132	3,634	174	66	77	383

	College							
8	Spring Hill College	6,461	109	7,694	147	81	128	384
8	Trinity College, Ill.	5,060	149	2,059	180	59	58	387
8	King College	2,913	183	13,118	119	69	85	387
8	Greenville College	5,033	150	7,066	155	68	83	388
8	Piedmont College	1,855	190	38,414	51	84	149	390
8	Wesleyan College	4,303	168	34,791	56	87	170	394
8	Warner Pacific College	5,360	145	892	189	61	61	395
8	Oglethorpe University	5,670	138	9,238	136	80	121	395
8	Thiel College	6,336	115	10,381	131	84	151	397
8	Emmanuel College	6,500	107	7,738	146	83	147	400
8	Warren Wilson College	6,270	117	19,310	98	92	185	400
8	Fisk University	4,251	169	4,890	166	63	67	402
8	Neumann College	5,994	126	2,915	177	74	101	404
9	Adrian College	6,093	123	12,513	124	86	165	412
9	Mary Baldwin College	5,201	146	15,581	112	85	160	418
9	Gordon College	6,915	87	5,816	162	88	172	421
9	Carroll College	5,408	144	7,197	152	81	127	423
9	MacMurray College	4,040	175	6,602	159	71	90	424
9	St. Mary-of-the-Woods	5,066	148	3,771	173	75	104	425
9	Blackburn College	3,109	179	12,895	121	81	125	425
9	Seton Hill College	6,232	118	6,507	160	84	152	430
9	Greensboro College	4,223	170	8,796	139	80	122	431
9	Luther College	6,616	102	7,255	150	91	181	433
9	Chestnut Hill College	4,190	171	2,977	176	70	87	434
9	Virginia Wesleyan College	6,053	124	5,726	164	83	146	434
9	Maryville College	4,438	163	13,321	117	85	156	436
9	Albertus Magnus College	7,549	74	1,760	185	92	183	442
9	Goshen College	5,698	136	10,423	130	91	182	448
9	Houghton College	5,899	131	7,100	154	86	164	449
9	Northland College	5,515	142	9,909	132	89	175	449
9	Bethel College, Kans.	3,994	176	17,828	101	89	174	451

Table A-2 (continued)

	Group and institution	Net tuition	Rank	Endowment	Rank	Percent of applicants accepted	Rank	Composite rank
10	Caldwell College	5,915	129	1,408	186	82	139	454
10	College of Mt. St. Vincent	6,343	113	1,011	188	84	154	455
10	Wartburg College	5,937	127	7,346	149	90	179	455
10	Dana College	4,075	173	4,807	167	79	116	456
10	Shorter College	4,052	174	13,054	120	86	162	456
10	Nebraska Wesleyan University	5,453	143	11,978	125	97	188	456
10	Bryan College	3,094	180	4,018	172	75	105	457
10	Thomas More College	4,751	158	4,232	170	83	143	471
10	Olivet College	4,790	155	7,832	145	94	186	486
10	Roberts Wesleyan College	5,913	130	2,022	183	89	176	489
10	Judson College, Ill.	5,025	151	7,066	156	97	187	494
10	Morris College	3,572	178	1,304	187	82	133	498
10	Claflin College	3,076	181	4,208	171	84	150	502
10	Bethel College, Tenn.	2,788	185	8,071	142	92	184	511
10	Jamestown College	2,410	188	7,651	148	90	180	516
10	Huntingdon College	2,735	186	4,750	168	87	169	523
10	Immaculata College	4,161	172	2,024	181	89	173	526
10	Judson College, Ala.	2,175	189	6,880	157	98	190	536
10	Barber-Scotia College	2,604	187	2,024	182	98	189	558

Source: Author's calculations based on data supplied by the College Board. New York, and the National Center for Higher Education Systems, Boulder, Colorado.
a. Net tuition and endowment in dollars calculated per full-time-equivalent student.

with high tuition may offer larger grants for each aided student, higher tuition levels generally yield larger amounts of net tuition revenue than would lower tuition levels because not all students receive aid.[11] (These relationships are explored in greater detail in chapter 3.) Finally, the ratio of acceptances to applications simply reveals the size of the applicant pool relative to the size of desired entering class, and is one measure of enrollment strength.[12]

Data for these three measures were computed for the 190 colleges for which they were available for academic year 1988-89, and each college was rank ordered on each measure from 1 to 190. The three rank orders were added together to produce a single composite ranking for each college, with the results presented in table A-2. Based on the composite measure, the colleges are arrayed in ten groups by descending financial and enrollment strength. Several of the analyses in chapters 3 and 4 use this ranking to assess economic trends in this sector during the 1980s.

11. The amount of endowed student aid a given college may have is partly the result of trustee decisions to dedicate unrestricted gifts to student aid. To that extent, the measure of net tuition revenue may understate the size of discounts for the better-endowed colleges.

12. Other measures, such as yield (the ratio of enrollments to acceptances) are plausible, but the ratio used is the most direct way of capturing the enrollment strength of a college in sheer numbers, without introducing qualitative considerations.

Colleges Excluded and Description of Williams College Data File

AS DISCUSSED in the text, more than 300 colleges classified by the Carnegie Foundation as Liberal Arts II were excluded from this study by the criterion that required at least 40 percent of their degrees awarded in 1985–86 be in arts and sciences fields. The following Liberal Arts I colleges were excluded because of graduate programs that make them essentially small universities: Antioch University; Bryn Mawr College; Bucknell University; Drew University; Hamline University; Lewis and Clark College; Radcliffe College; University of Dallas; Washington and Lee University; and Willamette University.

The following Liberal Arts II colleges met the criterion of having 40 percent or more of their degrees awarded in liberal arts and science fields but were excluded because enrollment in 1985–86 was less than 300: Borromeo College at Ohio (classified as a Liberal Arts I College); Burlington College; Christendom College; College of the Atlantic; Columbia College; Divine Word College; Howard Payne University; Mt. Vernon College (D.C.); Simons Rock of Bard College; Thomas Aquinas College; and World College West.

When the 40 percent criterion was applied to degree data for 1989–90, 14 Liberal Arts II colleges that met the criterion in 1985–86 failed to meet it four years later—these colleges are Barber-Scotia, Christ College, Christian Heritage, Flagler, Hawaii Loa, Jamestown, LeMoyne-Owen, Lourdes, Miles, Mount Ida, Palm Beach Atlantic, Piedmont, Roberts Wesleyan, and St. Mary-of-the-Woods. Five Liberal

Arts I colleges also failed to meet that criterion in 1989–90—Carroll, College of Mt. St. Vincent, Eckerd, MacMurray, and Wartburg.

The Williams College Data File

The data set consists of financial and other information on individual colleges and universities during the period from 1978–79 to 1988–89. It was constructed by merging three smaller data sets. One, the Financial Statistics report from the Higher Education General Information Survey (HEGIS) for the period up to 1985–86, and the Integrated Postsecondary Education Data System (IPEDS) for the more recent period, describes the basic financial accounts. The second, the Fiscal-Operations Report and Application to Participate (FISAP) data base, provides more detailed information on student aid spending and revenues, and on the aided population at colleges and universities who apply for federal assistance under any of the so-called campus-based programs (direct loans, supplementary educational opportunity grants [SEOGs], and college work study). The third, the HEGIS and IPEDS Enrollment Survey, reports full- and part-time enrollment for all institutions, allowing estimation of full-time-equivalent enrollment (FTE), which is used to express all of the financial data on a per-FTE-enrollment basis. All financial data are adjusted for inflation and are presented in 1990–91 dollars.[1]

1. Scott W. Blasdell, Michael S. McPherson, and Morton Owen Schapiro, "Trends in Revenues and Expenditures in U.S. Higher Education: Where Does the Money Come From? Where Does It Go?" Williams Project on the Economics of Higher Education, Williams College, Williamstown, Massachusetts, March 1992, pp. 1–2.

A Microeconomic Model

THE MICROECONOMIC model of a private college discussed in chapter 3 is presented in this appendix in a more formal manner. The discussion in the text that interprets the model is not repeated, and thus it may be helpful to refer again to chapter 3 for complete understanding.

The college seeks to maximize the value function:

$$V (X_Q, X_Q^* \mid X_N, X^*, P)$$

subject to a revenue constraint:

$$TR - TC \geq 0$$

where: X_Q = student quality (diversity)

X_Q^* = quality of input levels for X_N

X_N = desired enrollment level, for example,
      $1{,}150 \leq X_N \leq 1{,}250$

X^* = fixed input levels for X_N

P = tuition rate

TR = total revenue

TC = total cost

Figure 3-2 in chapter 3 presents the relationships among the posted tuition price, unfunded student aid, enrollment, and tuition revenue. Net tuition revenue (gross tuition revenue minus unfunded student aid) can be expressed in terms of figure 3-2 as the area $P\ a\ c\ X_N\ O$, or $(1 - \beta)\ P\ X_N$ algebraically.

An alternative specification for net tuition revenue can be expressed as the tuition price times the number of full-pay students, plus the sum of the individual prices paid by each of the aided students:

$$NTR = PX_{FP} + \sum_{i=FP}^{N} P_i X_i \tag{1}$$

define $\sum_{i=FP}^{N} P_i X_i = \overline{P} X_{PP}$ where

$\overline{P}$ = average tuition paid by students receiving aid (X_{PP})

substituting in (1):

$$NTR = PX_{FP} + \overline{P} X_{PP} \tag{2}$$

$$\text{but } X_{FP} = \alpha X_N$$

$$X_{PP} = (1 - \alpha) X_N$$

substituting in (2):

$$NTR = P\alpha X_N + \overline{P}(1 - \alpha) X_N \tag{3}$$

from figure 3-2, we know that

$$NTR = (1 - \beta) PX_N \tag{4}$$

equating (3) and (4), we have

$$(1 - \beta) PX_N = \alpha PX_N + (1 - \alpha) \overline{P} X_N \tag{5}$$

simplifying, and solving for β,

$$\beta = (1 - \alpha)(1 - \overline{P}/P) \tag{6}$$

Equation 6 states that the ratio of unfunded student aid to gross tuition revenue (β) equals the portion of students receiving unfunded aid ($1 - \alpha$) times the size of the average unfunded aid award ($1 - \overline{P}/P$).

To complete our economic theory of the private college, we must specify revenue and cost functions. A full specification of the total revenue (TR) function would be as follows:

$$TR = NTR + \mu E + G, \text{ where}$$

$$NTR = \text{net tuition revenue, } (1 - \beta) PX_N$$

$$E = \text{endowment}$$

$$\mu = \text{pay-out rate on endowment}$$

$$G = \text{other revenue (annual giving, and so on)}$$

The total cost (TC) function can be specified as follows:

$$TC = WX^*, \text{ where}$$

$$X^* = \text{input levels for enrollment } X_N$$

$$W = \text{a vector of wages (prices) paid for } X^*$$

There are three general cases governing the movement of cost as a function of enrollments:

$$TC = WX^* = K \text{ when } 1{,}150 \le X_N \le 1{,}250 \tag{1}$$

$$TC = WX^* + \epsilon X_{N-1250} \text{ when } X_N > 1{,}250 \tag{2}$$

$$TC = WX^* - \Delta X_{1150-N} \text{ when } X_N < 1{,}150 \tag{3}$$

The above set of cost functions assumes a desired enrollment level of 1,200; the terms ϵ and Δ are the short-run marginal costs of enrollments that fall outside the range of 1,150 to 1,250 enrollments, in this example.

Categories of Revenue and Expenditure

THE revenue categories are as follows:

Net revenue: The sum of net tuition revenue, gift and endowment income, federal, state and local grants and contracts, and state and local appropriations per FTE student.

Gross tuition and fee revenue per FTE student: The convention followed by academic institutions is to calculate this amount by assuming that every student pays the sticker or list price—hence this variable is gross of financial aid. Charges for room, board, and other services rendered by auxiliary enterprises are excluded.

Federal grants and contracts: Federal grants and contracts per FTE student minus Pell and supplemental educational opportunity grant amounts. Examples are research projects, training programs, and similar activities for which amounts are received or expenditures are reimbursable under the terms of a government grant or contract.

State and local grants and contracts per FTE student.

State and local appropriations per FTE student: Includes all amounts received or made available to an institution through acts of a legislative body, except grants of contracts. These funds are for meeting current operating expenses and not for specific projects or programs.

Gift and endowment income per FTE student: The sum of gifts to the endowment, gifts to the operating budget, realized and unrealized capital gains, interest, and dividends.

Net tuition and fee revenue per FTE student: The total amount of scholarship aid from institutional funds is subtracted from gross tuition and fees to calculate this net revenue figure.

Total scholarship aid from institutional funds per FTE student: I add scholarships and fellowships awarded from unrestricted and restricted funds and then subtract the financial aid contribution of the federal government, which is made in the form of Pell and SEOG grants.

Pell and SEOG grants: The sum of Pell and SEOG grants disbursed per FTE student. Administrative expenses are included for SEOG.

The expenditure categories are as follows:

Net spending per FTE student: I compute this number as the average value per FTE student of educational and general spending net of student aid. Student aid is netted out because part of this spending is directly "passed through" from federal student aid, and the rest is best seen as forgone institutional revenue, rather than as spending on educational programs.

Instruction and self-supported research per FTE student: Expenditures of the colleges, schools, departments, and other instructional divisions of the institution and expenditures for departmental research and public service that are not separately budgeted are included. Expenditures for academic administration where the primary function is administration (for example, academic deans) are excluded.

Research per FTE student: All funds expended for activities organized to produce research outcomes and commissioned by an agency external to the institution or separately budgeted by an organizational unit within the institution are included.

Public service per FTE student: This category includes all funds budgeted for public service and expended for activities established primarily to provide noninstructional services beneficial to groups external to the institution. Examples are seminars and projects provided to particular sectors of the community, community services, and cooperative extension projects.

Academic support per FTE student: Expenditures for the support services that are an integral part of the institution's primary missions of instruction, research, or public service are included. Expenditures for museums, galleries, audiovisual services, academic computing support, ancillary support, academic administration, personnel development, and course and curriculum development are examples.

I have taken out library expenditures and treated it as a separate category.

Library spending per FTE student: Expenditures on library.

Student services per FTE student: This category includes funds expended for admissions, registrar activities, and activities whose primary purpose is to contribute to students' emotional and physical well-being and to their intellectual, cultural, and social development outside the context of the formal instruction program. Examples are career guidance counseling, financial aid administration, student health services (except when operated as a self-supporting auxiliary enterprise), and the administrative allowance for Pell grants.

Institutional support per FTE student: Included are expenditures for the day-to-day operational support of the institution, excluding expenditures for physical plant operations. Examples are general administrative services, executive direction and planning, legal and fiscal operations, and community relations.

Operation and maintenance per FTE student: Includes all expenditures for operations established to provide service and maintenance related to campus grounds and facilities used for educational and general purposes. Expenditures made from institutional plant funds accounts are excluded.

Other spending per FTE student: This is the residual category, equal to the difference between net spending and the sum of the eight components.

Scholarships from restricted funds per FTE student: Included are scholarships and fellowships awarded from restricted funds, including Pell grants.

Scholarships from unrestricted funds per FTE student: Included are scholarships and fellowships awarded from unrestricted funds. This category, as well as the one above, applies only to moneys given in the form of outright grants and trainee stipends to individuals enrolled in formal course work, either for credit or not. Aid to students in the form of tuition or fee remissions is included (except those remissions granted because of faculty or staff status). College work study program expenses are reported where the student served, not in either of the scholarship categories.

Plant additions per FTE student: This is computed by summing over the three categories of physical plant additions during the year—land, buildings, and equipment. Additions during the year are additions to plant made through purchase, by gift-in-kind from donors, and from other additions. Construction in progress and plant expenditures that represent capital fund investments in real estate are excluded.

Administrators Interviewed

Bowdoin College
Robert H. Edwards, president
Charles R. Beitz, dean for academic affairs
Kent John Chabotar, vice president for finance and administration, and treasurer
William A. Torrey, vice president for development
Linda Kraemer, associate dean of admissions
Jane L. Jervis, dean of the college

Bradford College
Joseph Short, president
Peggy Maki, vice president and academic dean
Donald Kaszka, vice president for administration and finance
William A. Carey, vice president for institutional advancement
William Dunfey, dean of admissions

Colorado College
Gresham Riley, president (not interviewed)
Glenn Brooks, director of strategic planning
David D. Finley, dean of the college and dean of the faculty
Janice B. Cassin, vice president for business/finance and treasurer
Robert Mollenhauer, director of development
Elaine Freed, director of corporate, foundation and agency support
Terry K. Swenson, director of admissions and financial aid
Walter Hecox, professor of economics, and chair, faculty executive committee

Dickinson College
A. Lee Fritschler, president
George Allan, dean of the college

171

Michael L. Britton, treasurer

Robert O. White, executive director of communications and development

J. Larry Mench, dean of admissions and enrollment

Peter J. Balcziunas, assistant to the president

Fisk University

Henry Ponder, president

Ormond Smythe, dean of academic affairs

Linda Ellison, chief financial officer

Gerald T. Washington, director of development and university relations

Harrison F. DeShields, Jr., director of admissions

Guilford College

William R. Rogers, president

Daniel P. Poteet, provost

Kathrynn A. Adams, acting vice president for academic affairs/academic dean

James C. Newlin, vice president for finance and development

Richard L. Coe, business manager

Patricia R. McNeil, acting director of development

Larry West, director of admissions

Hollins College

Jane Margaret O'Brien, president

Joe W. Leedom, chair of the faculty

Timothy Hill, treasurer

James L. Hamlin, acting vice president for development and alumnae affairs

Anne Parry, dean of admissions and financial aid

Jane Bassett Spilman, chair, development committee, board of trustees

Knox College

John P. McCall, president

John R. Strassburger, dean of the college

Stephen Bailey, associate dean of the college

Lawrence W. Larson, vice president for finance and treasurer

Janet C. Hunter, dean of enrollment and institutional planning

Robert G. Kooser, professor of chemistry and chair, strategic planning committee

Olivet College
Donald A. Morris, president
B. Lee Cooper, academic vice president and dean of the college
Brian T. Cobb, chief financial officer
John O. McCandless, senior vice president
Timothy J. Nelson, vice president for enrollment and strategic management

Union College
Roger H. Hull, president
James E. Underwood, dean of the faculty and vice president for academic affairs
Diane T. Blake, comptroller
Robert B. Rasmussen, vice president for college resources
Daniel M. Lundquist, dean of admissions and financial aid

Westmont College
David K. Winter, president
George V. Blankenbaker, vice president/academic dean
Ronald W. Cronk, vice president for administration and finance
Glen W. Adams, vice president for college advancement
Joyce Brown Luy, associate director of admissions
Edwin J. Potts, assistant to the president

Wittenberg University
William A. Kinnison, president
Sammye Greer, provost
P. Gus Geil, vice president for business and finance
Michael J. Ferrin, vice president for university advancement
Charles A. Dominick, vice president for institutional relations
Kenneth G. Benne, dean of admissions

Index